AF520199

Competitive Exercises in

LIBRARY AND INFORMATION SCIENCE

(For Competitive Examinations)

Competitive Exercises in LIBRARY AND INFORMATION SCIENCE
(For Competitive Examinations)

HITESH GOPAL BRIJWASI
(B.LIB & Isc, BBM, DBM, M.lib & Isc, MBM, CBSE-UGC NET (LIS))
Librarian
Smt. Sharadchandrika Suresh Patil College of Pharmacy, Copda Dist Jalgaon.

Ess Ess Publications
New Delhi

PRESS:
THIS IS FOR THE HARDBOUND EDITION

Competitive Exercises in
LIBRARY AND INFORMATION SCIENCE
(For Competitive Examinations)

Copyright © by Author

All rights reserved. No part of this book may be reproduced in any form or by any electronic or mechanical means including information storage and retrieval systems without permission in writing from the publisher, except by a reviewer, who may quote brief passages in a review.

While extensive effort has gone into ensuring the reliability of information appearing in this book, the publisher makes no warranty, express or implied on the accuracy or reliability of the information, and does not assume and hereby disclaims any liability to any person for any loss or damage caused by errors or omissions in this publication.

ISBN : 978-81-936074-4-2

First Published 2018

Published by:
Ess Ess Publications
4831/24, Ansari Road,
Darya Ganj,
New Delhi-110 002.
INDIA
Phones: 23260807, 41563444
Fax: 41563334
E-mail: info@essessreference.com
www.essessreference.com

Cover Design by *Patch Creative Unit*

Printed and bound in India at Yash Printographics.

Dedicated to
MY PARENTS

Contents

॥ अंतरी पेटवू ज्ञानज्योत ॥

North Maharashtra University, Jalgaon

Umavinagar, Jalgaon - 425 001 (Maharashtra) INDIA

1990 'A' Grade NAAC Re-Accredited (3rd Cycle)

Prof. P. P. Patil
Ph.D., F.M.A.Sc.
VICE-CHANCELLOR

Foreword

The book '**Competitive Exercise in Library and Information Science'** is a humble attempt to guide the students from competitie examinations point of view. It is a good collection of MCQ questions related to Library and Information Science. Ten chapters of this book have been given in-depth coverage of all aspects that will definitely help the students to prepare for competitive examinations. This book is a comprehensive guide for the students, teachers, researchers and professionals of Library and Information Science.

I congratulate the author for his efforts in publishing this book.

My best wishes to the book **"Competitive Exercise in Library and Information Science".**

(Prof.P.P.Patil)
Vice-Chancellor

☎: (O)+91-257-2258401, 2258402, (R) +91-257-2258404, +91-257-2281978
Fax (O) : +91-257-2258403, (Mob.) : +91 9423185071, +91 9422215640
E-mail : vco@nmu.ac.in Web : www.nmu.ac.in

Acknowledgements

The sense of accomplishment of any task, is incomplete without mentioning names of those people who made it possible.

At the outset, I want to express my thanks to Hon'ble Prof. Dr. P. P. Patil, Vice-Chancellor, North Maharashtra University, Jalgaon (M.S.), India for giving his valuable "Foreword" and best wishes for the book.

I am also very thankful to the Entire Management of Smt. Sharadchandrika Suresh Patil College of Pharmacy and Prof. Dr. G. P. Vadnere, Principal, Smt. Sharadchandrika Suresh Patil college of Pharmacy, Chopda, (M.S, India) for motivating and supporting me for doing extra activities likes publications and research.

I shall always remain grateful to my parents for their unconditional love, support and encouragement. I wish to thank all my senior and respected colleagues from past & present without whose help this book would have not been written.

I am also thankful to all teaching and non-teaching staff of my college for their support and cooperation.

Finally, I would like to thank M/s Ess Ess Publications, New Delhi for bringing out the book with a attractive print and getup.

– Hitesh G. Brijwasi

NET EXAMINATION SCHEDULE
(As Per New Criteria)

APPLICABLE FROM DEC 2017

Session	*Paper*	*Marks*	*Number of Question*	*Duration*
First	I	100	50 questions all are compulsory (2 Marks for each questions)	1¼ Hours (09:30 A.M. to 10:45 A.M.)
Second	II	100	50 questions all are compulsory (2 Marks for each questions)	1¼ Hours (11:15 A.M. to 12:30 P.M.)
Third	III	150	75 questions all are compulsory (2 Marks for each questions)	2½ Hours (02:00 P.M. to 04:30 P.M.)

SET EXAMINATION CRITERIA

Session	*Paper*	*Number of Multiple Choice Questions*	*Marks*	*Duration*
First	I	60 out of which 50 questions are to be attempted	50 x 2 = 100	1¼ hours (10.00 a.m. to 11.15 a.m)
Second	II	50 questions all of which are compulsory	50 x 2 = 100	1¼ hours (11.45 a.m. to 01.00 p.m)
Third	III	75 questions all of which are compulsory	75 x 2 = 150	2½ hours (02.30 p.m. to 05.00 p.m)

1

Information, Communication and Society

1. The term communication came from which language
   (A) Greek (B) Latin
   (C) German (D) French
2. Now a day's what is a most important vital resource for societal development of a country?
   (A) Books (B) Knowledge
   (C) Information (D) Data
3. Which Indian university first started M.Lib & Isc & M.Phil cources
   (A) Delhi (B) Madras
   (C) SNDT, Mumbai (D) AMU, Aligarh
4. Which organization has introduced the concept of sister libraries for children and young adults reading
   (A) IFLA (B) LC
   (C) UNESCO (D) ILA
5. Khudabaksh Oriental library is situated at
   (A) Bhagalpur (B) Patna
   (C) Ranchi (D) Bhopal

6. Identify the association that has changed its original name:
   (A) ILA (B) SLA
   (C) LA (D) ALA
7. Information is a part of ...
   (A) Information Science
   (B) Scientific achievement
   (C) Knowledge
   (D) Communication
8. Raja Ramohan Roy Library foundation (RRRLF) was established to develop:
   (A) University Libraries (B) Digital Libraries
   (C) Public Libraries (D) Special Libraries
9. Data is plural form of ...
   (A) Datum (B) Date
   (C) Datas (D) Donnees
10. What does "Communication of Information" means?
    (A) Process of transmitting information
    (B) Process of disseminating information
    (C) Process of retrieval of information
    (D) Process of scanning information
11. The headquarters of Raja Ram Mohan Roy Library Foundation is situtated at
    (A) Delhi (B) Calcutta
    (C) Chennai (D) Nagpur
12. The first library Act in India was passed and implemented in
    (A) Maharashtra (B) Andhra Pradesh
    (C) Madras (D) Karnataka
13. The agency in India responsible for assigning ISSN is
    (A) The National Library
    (B) INSDOC (NASCAIR)

(C) INFLIBNET
(D) Raja Ram Mohan Roy Library Foundation

14. NATIS stands for
(A) National Information System
(B) National Technical Information System 3.
(C) National Team for Information Science 4.
(D) None of the above

15. European Translation Centre is located at
(A) Italy (B) France
(C) Netherland (D) Germany

16. An appropriate source to find out descriptive information is................ .
(A) Bibliography (B) Directory
(C) Encyclopedia (D) Dictionary

17. Full Name of Melvil Dewey
(A) Louis Melvil Dewey
(B) Kossuth Melvil Dewey
(C) Louis Kossuth Melvil Dewey
(D) Melvil Louis Kossouth Dewey

18. Library Week is celebrated on
(A) 10th November (B) 14th November
(C) 14th December (D) 25th December

19. Saraswathi Mahal Library is at
(A) Tanjore (B) Bhubaneswar
(C) Jaipur (D) Thiruvanathapuram

20. ILA was founded in 1933 at
(A) Bombay (B) Madras
(C) Delhi (D) Calcutta

21. Connema Public Library was established after the name of the then
(A) Governor (B) Judge
(C) King (D) Philanthropist

22. Invisible colleges are
   (A) networks of people interested in the same subject
   (B) help in communication
   (C) neither (A) nor (B)
   (D) both (A) and (B)

23. Propounder of 'Demand Theory' for the book selection is?
   (A) Colison (B) McColvin
   (C) Dr. S. R. Rangnathan (D) All of the above.

24. Which are the facets relating to INFLIBNET?
   (A) CALIBER (B) PLANNER
   (C) UGC-INFONET (D) SOUL
   Of these :
   (A) (a), (c) and (d) (B) (c), (b) and (a)
   (C) (a), (b) and (c) (D) all of these

25. Information may be categorised into
   (A) logical, analytical and statistical
   (B) statistical, descriptive and analytical
   (C) analytical, statistical and systematic
   (D) systematic, analytical and descriptive.

26. Information is ...
   (A) Raw data (B) Processed data
   (C) Input data (D) Organized data

27. The term intellectual Capital introduced by?
   (A) Peter Drucker (B) K. wiig
   (C) Stewart (D) Henry Fayol

28. What is Intellectual Property?
   (A) Books (B) All reading material
   (C) Intellectual thoughts (D) All of the above

29. The term "Information Service" is an improvised name...
   (A) Administration (B) Documentation
   (C) Bibliography (D) Reference service

30. ....is a process of Information
   (A) Books (B) CD-ROM
   (C) Computers (D) None of the above
31. The first Ph.d was awarded in 1957 to D.B. Krishna Rao from the university of delhi. Who was his guide?
   (A) Asa Don Dickinson (B) Rangnathan
   (C) W.A Bordon (D) None of the above
32. Which of the following is the example for Data?
   (A) Cotton (B) Yarn
   (C) Cloth (D) All of the above
33. Resource sharing is a part of ...
   (A) Library cooperation (B) Library administration
   (C) Library management (D) Library cataloguing
34. When was the American Library Association established?
   (A) 1876 (B) 1872
   (C) 1875 (D) 1880
35. DDC 22nd edition is published by
   (A) Forest Press (B) OCLC
   (C) IFLA (D) UNESCO.
36. The Chairman of the National Knowledge Commission, Govt. of India, is
   (A) D. P. Chattopadhyay (B) B. P. Barua
   (C) R. K. Dasgupta (D) Dr. Sam Pitroda
37. The marketing concepts in Library Servicc include
   (A) analysis, planning, implementation and control
   (B) advertising, planning, analysis and control
   (C) distribution, control, analysis, implementation
   (D) indexing, planning, control and implementation.
38. Which University appointed the first fulltime University Librarian in India
   (A) Delhi University (B) Calcutta University
   (C) Madras University (D) Punjab University

39. Raja Rammohan Roy Library Foundation:
    (i) Promotes public libraries
    (ii) Located at Mumbai
    (iii) Promotes school libraries
    (iv) Located at Kolkata
    Code :
    (A) (i) and (ii) are correct
    (B) (i) and (iv) are correct
    (C) (i) and (iii) are correct
    (D) (iii) and (iv) are correct
40. The Farmington plan is associated with:
    (A) Library Legislation
    (B) Library Cataloguing
    (C) Library Cooperation
    (D) Library Indexing Service
41. The "Principle of Literary Warrant"was propounded by:
    (A) S.R. Ranganathan (B) W. Hulme
    (C) Melvil Dewey (D) Derek De Solla Price
42. The National Library for the visually handicapped is located at:
    (A) Allahabad (B) Indore
    (C) Dehradun (D) Nainital
43. Informal Communication among knowledgeable persons is known as:
    (A) Invisible College
    (B) Information Gatekeeper
    (C) Communication Gatekeeper
    (D) Knowledge Management
44. UNESCO assisted Model Public Library in India is located at:
    (A) Kolkata (B) Delhi
    (C) Mumbai (D) Chennai

45. Mark the 'odd one out':
    (A) Cow-Calf principle
    (B) Principle of osmosis
    (C) Wall picture principle
    (D) Whole organ principle

46. The office of patent information system in India is at
    (A) Mumbai (B) New Delhi
    (C) Kolkata (D) Nagpur

47. 'Noise' in Information Retrieval is due to............. .
    (A) Precision
    (B) Recall
    (C) Relevant information
    (D) Redundant information

48. National Medical Library (NML) of India is located at:
    (A) Mumbai (B) New Delhi
    (C) Calcutta (D) Chennai

49. Library of Congress is located at
    (A) Washington D.C (B) Chicago
    (C) New York (D) London

50. Match the following :

List-I	List-II
(a) Nehru Memorial Museum Library	(i) Chennai
(b) Connemara Public Library	(ii) Pune
(c) Bhandarkar Oriental Research Institute Library	(iii) Patna
(d) Khudabaksh Oriental Library	(iv) Delhi
	(v) Allahabad

Code :	**(a)**	**(b)**	**(c)**	**(d)**
(A)	(iii)	(v)	(iv)	(ii)
(B)	(v)	(iv)	(i)	(ii)
(C)	(v)	(ii)	(iv)	(i)
(D)	(iv)	(i)	(ii)	(iii)

51. The concept "Invisible College" first used by :
    (A) Eugene Garfield (B) Derek Solla Price
    (C) Allent Kent (D) Carl Savage

52. Match the following :

	List-I	List-II
(a)	IFLA	(i) Science Citation Index
(b)	Unesco	(ii) First search
(c)	OCLC	(iii) Patent Information
(d)	ISI	(iv) Public Library Manifesto
		(v) Universal Availability of Publications

Code :	**(a)**	**(b)**	**(c)**	**(d)**
(A)	(iii)	(iv)	(ii)	(i)
(B)	(iv)	(iii)	(i)	(ii)
(C)	(v)	(iv)	(ii)	(i)
(D)	(v)	(i)	(iv)	(ii)

53. IFLA took up the "Universal Availability of Publication" program in the year.............. .
    (A) 1973 (B) 1976
    (C) 1972 (D) 1970

54. International Information System on Research in Documentation (ISORID) was established by :
    (A) IFLA (B) UNESCO
    (C) SLA (D) ALA

55. The journal "Knowledge Organization" is published by :
    (A) IFLA (B) ISKO
    (C) LA (D) LC

56. Who publishes Annals of Library Science and documentation?
    (A) ILA (B) INSDOC (now NISCAIR)
    (C) DRTC (D) IASLIC

57. Identify the correct chronological order in which the following were established:

(A) National Library of India (Kolkata), Delhi Public Library, Documentation Research and Training Centre, Raja Ram Mohan Roy Library Foundation

(B) Delhi Public Library, Documentation Research and Training Centre, Raja Ram Mohan Roy Library Foundation, National Library of India (Kolkata)

(C) Documentation Research and Training Centre, Raja Ram Mohan Roy Library Foundation, National Library of India (Kolkata), Delhi Public Library

(D) Raja Ram Mohan Roy Library Foundation, National Library of India (Kolkata), Delhi Public Library, Documentation Research and Training Centre

58. Match the following :

List-I	**List-II**
(a) ERNET	(i) Japan
(b) JANET	(ii) Global
(c) RLIN	(iii) India
(d) OCLC	(iv) United Kingdom
	(v) USA

Code :	**(a)**	**(b)**	**(c)**	**(d)**
(A)	(v)	(iv)	(i)	(ii)
(B)	(iv)	(v)	(i)	(ii)
(C)	(iii)	(iv)	(v)	(ii)
(D)	(iii)	(ii)	(iv)	(v)

59. The head quarter of IASLIC are located at

(A) Calcutta (B) Bombay

(C) Chennai (D) Banglore

60. "Special libraries serve a specialist clientele, located within a single establishment or group and all engaged in working towards one common purpose." Who said this

(A) R.Astall (B) UNESCO
(C) J.D.Brown (D) E.C.Richardson

61. When RRRLF was established?
(A) 1970 (B) 1971
(C) 1972 (D) 1974

62. Where is the headquarter of RRRLF?
(A) Banglore (B) Delhi
(C) Calcutta (D) Lucknow

63. Who provides the ISBN?
(A) Niscair (B) Nissat
(C) Insdoc (D) RRRLF

64. Connemera Public Library is the State Central Library of
(A) Kerala (B) Karnataka
(C) Andhra Pradesh (D) Tamil Nadu

65. The CCF was developed by
(A) LC (B) UNESCO
(C) IFLA (D) FID

66. POPSI was developed by
(A) S.R. Ranganathan (B) Neelmeghan
(C) B.S. Kesavan (D) G. Bhattacharya

67. The real name of 'Mark Twain' is
(A) Milton
(B) Keats
(C) Samuel Longhorne Clemens
(D) William Wordsworth

68. C.L.R.I (Central Leather Research Institute) is located at
(A) Chennai (B) Calicut
(C) Cochin (D) Cuttack

69. Of the following libraries in India, which one is the oldest library?

(A) Asiatic Society Library, Bombay
(B) Connemara public Library, Madras
(C) Delhi Public Library, Delhi
(D) National Library of India, Calcutta

70. Noise in information retrieval is due to
(A) Precision
(B) Recall
(C) Relevant Information
(D) Redundant Information

71. Which library first introduced the printed catalog
(A) British Museum (B) Library of Congress
(C) Lelin State (D) Imperial Library

72. Informal self education is possible in what kind of library?
(A) National Library (B) Public Library
(C) Specific Library (D) College Library

73. The headquarters of Raja Ram Mohan Roy Library Foundation is situated at
(A) Delhi (B) Calcutta
(C) Chennai (D) Nagpur

74. The concept of UBC was introduced by
(A) UNESCO (B) LC
(C) FID (D) IFLA

75. GOC helps libraries in determining
(A) foreign exchange rates
(B) names of foreign agents and vendors
(C) books available in the market
(D) which books to buy

76. In a library which of the following positions are line positions
(i) Junior library assistant
(ii) Subject Specialist
(iii) Deputy Librarian
(iv) Systems Librarians

Codes :

(A) (i) and (ii) (B) (i) and (iii)

(C) (i) and (iv) (D) (ii) and (iv)

77. "Fair use" is a term most relevant to:

(A) Intellectual Property Right

(B) Books borrowed for home reading

(C) Copyright

(D) Use of reference books

78. which of the following is not a national library?

(A) Library of Congress

(B) British Library

(C) Bibliotheque Nationale

(D) Smithsonian Institute

79. UNESCO's Public Library Manifesto was last revised in

(A) 1990 (B) 1998

(C) 1997 (D) 1994

80. The oldest and the largest Library Association in the world is .

(A) ALA (B) LA

(C) IFLA (D) IASLIC

81. Which of the following is not covered under Intellectual Property Rights?

(A) Copyrights (B) Patents

(C) Trade Marks (D) Thesaurus

82. Chairman of National Knowledge Commission is.

(A) Pranab Mukherjee (B) Nandan Nilekani

(C) P. Chidambaram (D) Sam Pitroda

83. Which is not language barrier

(A) Neologism (B) Synonym

(C) Antonym (D) Propaganda

84. Currently "Science Citation Index" is published by.

(A) Emerald (B) Springer
(C) Thomson (D) Elsevier

85. Which of the following is an 'Acronym'?
(A) UNESCO (B) UNO
(C) UNDP (D) UGC

86. A set of rules that govern overall data communications system is popularly known as
(A) Protocol (B) Agreement
(C) Pact (D) Memorandum

87. Staffing is concerned with providing and maintaining .... resources.
(A) Physical (B) Technical
(C) Human (D) Financial

88. Match the following and choose the correct answer from the codes given below :

	List A		**List B**
(1)	Asiatic Society Library	a.	Kolkata
(2)	Connemara Public Library	b.	Chennai
(3)	Khuda Bux Oriental Library	c.	Patna
(4)	Saraswati Mahal Library	d.	Tanjore.

Codes :	**1**	**2**	**3**	**4**
(A)	a	b	c	d
(B)	d	a	b	c
(C)	c	d	a	b
(D)	b	d	a	c

89. Match the following and choose the correct answer from the codes given below :

	List A	**List B**
(1)	World of learning	a. Alphabetical
(2)	Sear's list of subject headings	b. Classified
(3)	Roget's International Thesaurus	c. Geographical
(4)	Indian National Bibliography	d. Topical.

Codes:	**1**	**2**	**3**	**4**
(A)	b	d	a	c
(B)	c	a	d	b
(C)	a	b	c	d
(D)	d	a	b	c

90. Whether Library is a system?
    (A) Yes, it has various sections as sub-systems coordinating each other forming a system
    (B) No, it cannot be a system
    (C) It is quite impossible
    (D) Library is separate from a system.

91. In which year did A. W. Borden start a refresher course for librarians in India?
    (A) 1905 (B) 1910
    (C) 1912 (D) 1913.

92. The first to introduce M.Phil programme in Library and Information Science in 1980 is
    (A) University of Delhi
    (B) Punjab University
    (C) Banaras Hindu University
    (D) Calcutta University

93. In which year was the International Book Year celebrated by UNESCO?
    (A) 1931 (B) 1947
    (C) 1952 (D) 1972.

94. What is the full form of IATLIS?
    (A) International Association of Trade Unions of Library Science
    (B) Indian Association of Teachers in Library & Information Science
    (C) Indian Airlines Technical Lower Intelligence Services
    (D) Indian Air Traffic Light, Information and Signal.

95. Management by Objectives (MBO) is introduced by
(A) H. W. Wilson (B) S. R. Ranganathan
(C) F. W. Taylor (D) Peter Drucker.

96. IIA founded in U.S.A. in 1968 stands for
(A) Integrated Industry Association
(B) Information Industry Association
(C) Integrated Illiteracy eradication Association
(D) Institute of Information Association.

97. Who devised the motto of ALA
(A) S. R. Rangnathan (B) J. D. Brown
(C) Melvil Dewey (D) C.A Cutter

98. The first centre to use computer in the library and information activities in India is
(A) DESIDOC (B) INSDOC
(C) DRTC (D) UGC.

99. The Library Committee apointed by the UGC in 1957 was headed by
(A) PN Kaula (B) B. S. Kesavan
(C) S. R. Rangnathan (D) K. P. Sinha

100. Name of the person who was appointed as first fulltime university librarian in india?
(A) A Dickinson (B) Web Sayers
(C) B. S. Kesavan (D) Harinath De

101. Calcutta Public Library was established during
(A) 15th Century (B) 16th Century
(C) 19th Century (D) 20th Century.

102. Linear model of communication in knowledge based on Aristotles' model of communication was proposed by
(A) Juger Heberman
(B) A.J. Wells
(C) C.E. Shannon & W. Weaver
(D) G. Gerbner

103. Effective communication is essentially a
   (A) One way Process
   (B) Two Way Process
   (C) Both one way and two way process
   (D) Three way process

104. IASLIC was founded in the year
   (A) 1955 (B) 1965
   (C) 1975 (D) 1985

105. UNIMARC was developed under the umbrella of
   (A) OCLC (B) IFLA
   (C) UNESCO (D) None of the above

106. Arrange the following States according to the year of enactment of library legislation:
   (I) Pondicherry (II) Orissa
   (III) Rajasthan (IV) Karnataka

   Codes :
   (A) (IV), (I), (III), (II) (B) (IV), (II), (III), (I)
   (C) (IV), (III), (I), (II) (D) (I), (III), (II), (IV)

107. Arrange the following chronologically according to their year of Birth:
   (I) S.R. Ranganathan (II) Melvil Dewey
   (III) C.A. Cutter (IV) B.S. Kesvan

   Codes :
   (A) (II), (I), (IV), (III) (B) (I), (III), (IV), (II)
   (C) (III), (II), (I), (IV) (D) (IV), (I), (II), (III)

108. Match the following :

List – I	**List – II**
(a) Books in print	(i) Bibliography of periodicals
(b) Ulrich International Periodical Directory	(ii) Trade Bibliography
(c) World of Learning	(iii) Biographical source
(d) Who's Who in India	(iv) Directory

Code :	**(a)**	**(b)**	**(c)**	**(d)**
(A)	(ii)	(i)	(iv)	(iii)
(B)	(i)	(ii)	(iii)	(iv)
(C)	(iii)	(i)	(iv)	(ii)
(D)	(i)	(iii)	(iv)	(ii)

109. Match the following :

List – I	**List – II**
(a) E.J. Coates	(i) KWIC
(b) H.P. Luhn	(ii) Things, Property, Material, Action
(c) Derek Austin	(iii) Concrete and process
(d) J. Kaiser	(iv) PRECIS

Code :	**(a)**	**(b)**	**(c)**	**(d)**
(A)	(i)	(ii)	(iii)	(iv)
(B)	(ii)	(i)	(iv)	(iii)
(C)	(iii)	(ii)	(i)	(iv)
(D)	(iv)	(i)	(ii)	(iii)

110. Match the following :

List – I	**List – II**
(a) NTC	(i) UK
(b) ITC	(ii) India
(c) BLDSC	(iii) Netherlands
(d) NISCAIR	(iv) USA

Code :	**(a)**	**(b)**	**(c)**	**(d)**
(A)	(iv)	(iii)	(i)	(ii)
(B)	(ii)	(i)	(iv)	(iii)
(C)	(i)	(iii)	(ii)	(iv)
(D)	(i)	(ii)	(iii)	(iv)

111. As per Indian Copyright Law, copyright is granted for
(A) Fifty years after the book is published
(B) Fifty years after the death of the author
(C) Sixty years after the book is published
(D) Sixty years after the death of the author

112. NAAC stands for
(A) National Accreditation and Authority Council
(B) Northern Accreditation and Authorities Committee
(C) National Assessment and Accreditation Council
(D) Northern Assessment and Accreditation Council

113. Who is the Father of Library Movement in USA?
(A) F. W. Lancaster (B) Paul Wasserman
(C) Melvil Dewey (D) Allen Kent

114. New Encyclopaedia Britannica is published from
(A) London (B) New York
(C) Paris (D) Chicago

115. Which of the following is not characteristic of information?
(A) Dynamic
(B) Contain in subject realm
(C) Unstructured
(D) Basis for action

116. All Union Institute for Scientific and Technical Information (VINITI) was established in
(A) 1952 (B) 1953
(C) 1954 (D) 1956

117. **Assertion (A) :** Information Literacy provides training to use maximum resources available in a library.

Reason (R) : Information Literacy always aims at specific group of users. Codes :

Codes :
(A) (A) is false, but (R) is true.
(B) Both (A) and (R) are false.
(C) Both (A) and (R) are true.
(D) (A) is true, but (R) is false.

118. **Assertion (A) :** Performance measurement is necessary to support decision making in libraries and information centres.

Reason (R) : Right decision at a right time helps libraries and information centres to achieve goals.

Codes :

(A) Both (A) and (R) are true and (R) is the correct explanation of (A).

(B) Both (A) and (R) are false.

(C) Both (A) and (R) are true, but (R) is not a correct explanation of (A).

(D) (A) is false, but (R) is true.

119. Oral Communication is also known as

(A) Verbal Communication

(B) Non Verbal Communication

(C) Formal Communication

(D) Informal of the above

120. Which of the following professional Associations does not exist now?

(A) IFLA (B) FID

(C) ALA (D) IASLIC

121. Which of the following is not considered as data?

(A) Letters (B) Symbols

(C) Words (D) Message

122. Identify the correct order as per year of establishment

(i) ASLIB (ii) IATLIS

(iii) SLA (iv) ALA

Codes :

(A) (iv), (iii), (i), (ii) (B) (iv), (ii), (i), (iii)

(C) (ii), (i), (iv), (iii) (D) (i), (ii), (iii), (iv)

123. Arrange the following in chronological order:

(i) Fayzee Committee
(ii) K. P. Sinha Committee
(iii) Chattopadhyaya Committee
(iv) Radhakrishnan Committee

Codes :

(A) (i), (ii), (iii), (iv) (B) (iv), (iii), (i), (ii)
(C) (i), (iv), (ii), (iii) (D) (iii), (i), (ii), (iv)

124. Arrange the following States chronologically according to year of enactment of Library Legislation.

(i) Tamil Nadu (ii) U.P.
(iii) Gujarat (iv) Mizoram

Codes :

(A) (iv), (iii), (i), (ii) (B) (ii), (iv), (iii), (i)
(C) (i), (iv), (iii), (ii) (D) (i), (ii), (iv), (iii)

125. Match the following

	List – I		List – II
(a)	Best books for the largest numbers	(i)	D.B.Krishna Rao
(b)	Library is the heart of all university work	(ii)	B.S. Kesavan
(c)	First Ph.D. in Library Science	(iii)	S. Radhakrishnan
(d)	First Librarian of National Library (India)	(iv)	MelvilDewey

Code :	(a)	(b)	(c)	(d)
(A)	(i)	(ii)	(iii)	(iv)
(B)	(iv)	(iii)	(ii)	(i)
(C)	(iii)	(iv)	(i)	(ii)
(D)	(iv)	(iii)	(i)	(ii)

126. Arrange the following professional Associations according to the year of their establishment :

(i) ILA (ii) IASLIC
(iii) ALA (iv) ASLIB

Codes :

(A) (i), (ii), (iii), (iv) (B) (iii), (iv), (i), (ii)
(C) (iv), (iii), (ii), (i) (D) (i), (iii), (ii), (iv)

127. Match the following :

List - I	**List - II**
(a) SENDOC	(i) Social Sciences
(b) INPADOC	(ii) Sciences
(c) NASSDOC	(iii) Patents
(d) INSDOC (NISCAIR)	(iv) Small Scale Industries

Code :	**(a)**	**(b)**	**(c)**	**(d)**
(A)	(ii)	(iii)	(iv)	(i)
(B)	(i)	(ii)	(iii)	(iv)
(C)	(iv)	(iii)	(i)	(ii)
(D)	(iii)	(iv)	(i)	(ii)

128. Match the following :

List - I (Subjects)	**List - II (Modes of Formation)**
(a) India	(i) Agglomeration
(b) Agriculture of wheat	(ii) Lamination
(c) Biochemistry	(iii) Fusion
(d) Biological Sciences	(iv) Denudation

Code :	**(a)**	**(b)**	**(c)**	**(d)**
(A)	(iv)	(ii)	(iii)	(i)
(B)	(i)	(iii)	(ii)	(iv)
(C)	(iv)	(iii)	(i)	(ii)
(D)	(ii)	(iv)	(iii)	(i)

129. Match the following :

List - I	List - II
(a) The Right to Information Act of India	(i) 2000
(b) Universal Declaration of Human Rights	(ii) 2005
(c) Information Technology Act. (India)	(iii) 1948
(d) Digital Millennium Act	(iv) 1998

Code :	(a)	(b)	(c)	(d)
(A)	(i)	(ii)	(iii)	(iv)
(B)	(ii)	(iii)	(i)	(iv)
(C)	(iii)	(ii)	(iv)	(i)
(D)	(iv)	(iii)	(ii)	(i)

130. Match the following :

List - I	List - II
(a) NASSDOC	(i) Defence Science
(b) DEVSIS	(ii) Social Sciences
(c) INIS	(iii) Development Science
(d) DESIDOC	(iv) NuclearScience

Code :	(a)	(b)	(c)	(d)
(A)	(iv)	(ii)	(i)	(iii)
(B)	(ii)	(iii)	(iv)	(i)
(C)	(i)	(ii)	(iii)	(iv)
(D)	(iii)	(ii)	(i)	(iv)

131. Match the following :

List - I	List - II
(a) Father of Scientific Management	(i) Henry Fayol
(b) Father of Administration	(ii) Elton Mayo
(c) Father of Human Relations School	(iii) F. Hertzberg
(d) Father of Corporate Strategy	(iv) F.W. Taylor

Code :	**(a)**	**(b)**	**(c)**	**(d)**
(A)	(iv)	(ii)	(i)	(iii)
(B)	(iv)	(i)	(ii)	(iii)
(C)	(iii)	(iv)	(ii)	(i)
(D)	(ii)	(iii)	(iv)	(i)

132. The University which telecasts interaction educational programmes through its own channel is
    (A) Osmania University
    (B) University of Pune
    (C) Annamalai University
    (D) Indira Gandhi National Open University (IGNOU)

133. Which of the following skills are needed for present day teacher to adjust effectively with the classroom teaching?
    (A) Knowledge of technology
    (B) Use of technology in teaching learning
    (C) Knowledge of students' needs
    (D) Content mastery

    Codes:
    (A) 1 & 3 (B) 2 & 3
    (C) 2, 3 & 4 (D) 2 & 4

134. who has signed an MOU for Accreditation of Teacher Education Institutions in India?
    (A) NAAC and UGC (B) NCTE and NAAC
    (C) UGC and NCTE (D) NCTE and IGNOU

135. National Library Week in India is being celebrated annually since:
    (A) 1914 (B) 1933
    (C) 1950 (D) 1968

136. Maulana Abul Kalam Azad, the then Union Education Minister formally declared one of the following libraries open to the public on 2nd February, 1953 :

(A) Connemara Public Library
(B) Delhi Public Library
(C) National Library, Calcutta
(D) Saraswathi Mahal Library, Tanjore

137. Culcutta Piblic Library was designated as imperial library by
(A) William Bentinct (B) Lord Curzon
(C) Lord Minto (D) Lord Welesly

138. A. Issac Collijin was the first president of IFLA
B. "Tree of porphyry" is formed as a result of Polychotonomy
(A) A only Correct (B) B only correct
(C) A & B are correct (D) None is correct

139. Who designated Dr.Ranganathan as "father of library science"?
(A) Jawaharlal Nehru (B) Sir Radhakrishnan
(C) Rajendra Prasad (D) Sir Maurice Gwoyer

140. A.Sokteo is called as Dewey of Japan B.Benjamin A Custor was the editor of AARC II
(A) A only Correct (B) B only correct
(C) A&B are correct (D) None is correct

141. A.Borden introduced Open Access System in India B.The concept of "anamolous state of knowledge " was proposed by Dr.Ranganathan
(A) A only Correct (B) B only correct
(C) A&B are correct (D) None is correct

142. How many national library in Italy?
(A) 4 (B) 8
(C) 12 (D) 16

143. A. The concept "Technological Gate Keepers" was first proposed by Allen
B. UNISIST is a collobaritive product of UNESCO and IFLA

Code :

(A) A only Correct (B) B only correct
(C) A&B are correct (D) None is correct

144. UGC was founded in 1953 B.UNESCO was founded in 1951

(A) A only Correct (B) B only correct
(C) A & B are correct (D) None is correct

145. A.India Office Library is situated in New Delhi B."Library is the heart of an institution" said by S.R.Ranganathan

(A) A only Correct (B) B only correct
(C) A & B are correct (D) None is correct

146. Data is …

(A) Qualitative (B) Quantitative
(C) Both (A) and (B) (D) Neither (A) or (B)

147. Rangnathan designed ____ method of deriving subject heading for documents

(A) Book Index Entry (B) BList of subject Entry
(C) Chain Procedure (D) Subject Index Entry

148. Informal communication among knowledgeable person is known as:

(A) Invisible College
(B) Information Gatekeeper
(C) Communication Gatekeeper
(D) Knowledge Management

149. The transmission of receivers reaction to back to the sender is known as-

(A) Noise (B) Feedback
(C) Medium (D) Source

150. The Mathematical theory of communication was first developed by

(A) Warren Weaver (B) Claude Shannon
(C) Cherry (D) Osgood

151. Connemera Public Library is the state Central Libray of
   (A) Kerala (B) Madras
   (C) Karnataka (D) Tamilnadu
152. Where is the head quarter of Patent Information System in India.
   (A) Pune (B) Mumbai
   (C) Nagpur (D) Delhi
153. what is the unit of information?
   (A) Bit (B) Byte
   (C) Gram (D) Hertz
154. UNISIST is a
   (A) Software (B) A Programme
   (C) Welfare association (D) A committee
155. Which association's tagline is "managing information"?
   (A) IFLA (B) Aslib
   (C) ALA (D) LC
156. When did ILA became the member of IFLA?
   (A) 1952 (B) 1955
   (C) 1957 (D) 1965
157. Which association's tagline is "connecting people and information"?
   (A) SLA (B) IFLA
   (C) ALA (D) COMLA
158. Which organization has introduced the concept of "Sister libraries" for children's and young adults reading?
   (A) UNESCO (B) IFLA
   (C) LC (D) LA
159. Who said that "Librarianship is not a profession"?
   (A) Madden, Moon, Moore, Mc Pheron
   (B) Goode, Rossi, Shaffer, Gullis
   (C) Dewey, Rundey, Reeves, Aishen
   (D) Ranganathan, Dewey, Cutter

160. Which organization was joined with Library Association to form CILIP in 2002?
    (A) Institute of Bibliography
    (B) Institute of Information Scientists
    (C) Institute of Documentation
    (D) Institute of Librarianship
161. in which year headquarter of FID was shifted from Brussels to The Hague?
    (A) 1925 (B) 1928
    (C) 1930 (D) 1934
162. Where was the first library noticed in India?
    (A) Taxila (B) Nalanda
    (C) Vallabhi (D) Sravasti
163. when was the curriculam development committee on LIS instituted?
    (A) 1988-89 (B) 1990-93
    (C) 1994-97 (D) 1999-02
164. Which association in India awards teachers in LIS?
    (A) IATLIS (B) ILA
    (C) IASLIC (D) SIS
165. where is the head quarter of SLA?
    (A) New York (B) Lagos
    (C) Shimla (D) New Delhi
166. when was the Amercian Library Assoication established
    (A) 1876 (B) 1872
    (C) 1875 (D) 1880
167. The Librarian Day celebrated on
    (A) 15th Sep (B) 24th Nov
    (C) 11th Dec (D) 12th Aug
168. The first library school was started by

(A) Melvin Dewey
(B) Charles Williamson
(C) John Macfarlane
(D) William Allenson Borden

169. who defined notation as shorthand sign
(A) Dr. S. R. Ranganathan
(B) Benjamin A. Custer
(C) Immanuel Kant
(D) E. C. Richardson

170. who enunciated the five fundamental categories
(A) Benjamin A. Custer
(B) Paul Otlet
(C) Dr. S. R. Ranganathan
(D) W. C. Sayers

171. "POSDCORB" coined by
(A) Peter F. Drucker (B) Harold Koontz
(C) F.W. Taylor (D) Luther Gulick

172. When Peter F. Drucker defined M.B.O. (Management by Objectives)?
(A) 1950 (B) 1960
(C) 1954 (D) 1964

173. who said the demand and supply theory of books?
(A) Melvil Dewey (B) Dr. S. R. Ranganathan
(C) Mc Colvin (D) Sayers

174. "To provide the best books to the maximum readers at the least cost" said by
(A) Dr.S.R. Ranganathan (B) P. N. Kaula
(C) E.Mayo (D) Melvil Dewey

175. Which national agency in India is responsible for assigning the ISBN
(A) RRRLF (B) BARC
(C) NCL (D) National Library of India

176). Zero Base Budgeting system was propounded by

(A) Peter F. Drucker (B) P.N. Kaula

(C) E.Mayo (D) Pter Phyrr

177. When Zero Base Budgeting system was first prepared

(A) 1950 (B) 1960

(C) 1970 (D) 1980

178. Posting the right person at the right place is called ________

(A) Recruitment (B) Coaching

(C) Deployment (D) Induction

179. Who is the pioneer of open access system in British libraries

(A) Nine e.Brown (B) James Duff Brown

(C) John cotton dana (D) S. R. Ranganathan

180. A good library building is an outcome of librarian and _________.

(A) Registrar (B) Building Corporation

(C) Finance Officer (D) Architect

181. Information Gatekeepers come under _____ sources.

(A) documentary

(B) human

(C) institutional

(D) neo-conventional

182. Which library is authorized to receive books under 'Delivery of Books Act'?

(A) National Science Library, Delhi

(B) Central Library, Delhi

(C) State Central Library, Mumbai

(D) Parliament Library, Delhi

183. The head office of Indian Library Association (ILA) is

(A) Delhi (B) Kolkata

(C) Bengalore (D) Mumbai

184. Shannon and Weaver related to
 (A) Psycho-biology of language An introduction to dynamic philosophy
 (B) Information is data of value to decision making
 (C) Mathematical Theory of Information
 (D) Bradford's Law of Information

185. The Head Office of UNESCO located at
 (A) Paris, France
 (B) Netherlands, in The Hague
 (C) London
 (D) England

186. The head office of Good Offices Committee is at
 (A) Kolkata (B) New Delhi
 (C) Bangalore (D) Chennai

187. An Invisible college is a typical example of
 (A) Informal channels of communication
 (B) Formal channels of communication
 (C) Both (A) and (B)
 (D) None of the above

188. The Library Association (UK) is now the component of
 (A) ASLIB (B) CILIP
 (C) ALA (D) None of the above

189. INSDOC has been merged with NISCOM and is now known as
 (A) DELNET (B) NISCAIR
 (C) DESIDOC (D) NASSDOC

190. Handling of Information in the sense of production is called
 (A) Information Marketing
 (B) Information Industry
 (C) Information Production
 (D) Information Revolution

191. which one of the following is not associated with the communication system?

(A) Receiver (B) Channel

(C) Sender (D) Entropy

192. The invisible web refers to-

(A) The internet, since we cannot see it

(B) That part of the internet, which is hidden from the search engines

(C) The telecommunication signals which are not seen

(D) The failure in accessing the web pages

193. who was the chairman of National Library Committee of India?

(A) B. S. Jha (B) K. P. Sinha

(C) S. Mudaliar (D) C. D. Deshmukh

194. which organisation applied Library and Information Policy in India at national level.

(A) NISSAT (B) INSDOC

(C) UNESCO (D) RRRLF

195. To which country the credit is given to coin the term information society?

(A) USA (B) France

(C) Japan (D) India

196. Today information is regarded as which of the following?

(A) Wealth (B) Commodity

(C) Products (D) All the above

197. LA is the Library Association of

(A) Manipur (B) Andhra Pradesh

(C) Great Britain (D) Canada.

198. Of the following libraries in India, which one is the oldest library?

(A) Asiatic Society Library, Bombay
(B) Connemara Public Library, Madras
(C) Delhi Public Library, Delhi
(D) National Library of India, Calcutta

199. Raw, unevaluated, unprocessed and unorganized facts is known as
(A) Data (B) Information
(C) Knowledge (D) Wisdom

200. When ERNET is established?
(A) 1988 (B) 1986
(C) 1990 (D) 1992

201. "It is a library with little or no physical presence of books, periodicals, reading space or support staff, but are that disseminate disseminate selective information directly to distribute library customers, usually electronically". Said by whom?
(A) Kay Gapen (B) Powell
(C) Sherwell (D) H. G. Wells

202. "A library is a public institution or establishment charged with the care of collection of books, the duty of making them accessible to those who require the use of them and the task of converting every person in its neighborhood into a habitual library goers and reader of books."Quoted by whom?
(A) Dr S R Ranganathan (B) K.N.Raj
(C) C.A.Cutter (D) W.C.Sayers

203. which is correct logical sequence of the following.
(A) Information, Knowledge, Data, Wisdom
(B) Knowledge, Wisdom, Information, Data
(C) Wisdom, Information, Data, Knowledge
(D) Data, Infomation, Knowledge, Wisdom

204. SMCR Communication model was developed by

(A) David K Berlo (B) Harold Lasswell
(D) Charles Osgood (C) W. Schramm

205. Identiify the correct sequence of user tasks that are supported by the structured of FRBR, RDA 0.2 version
(A) Identify, Select, Obtain, Find
(B) Find, Indentify, Select, Obtain
(C) Select, Identify, Find, Obtain
(D) Find, Select, Identify, Obtain

206. Which of the following are formal means of communication
(i) Adhoc talks (ii) Report
(iii) Blogs (iv) Meetings
Codes :
(A) (i), (ii) and (iii) are correct
(B) (ii) and (iii) are Coreect
(C) (ii) and (iv) are correct
(D) (i), (ii) and (iv) are correct

207. which of the following elements are associated with Dervins Model of Information Seeking Behaviour?
(i) Situation (ii) Extracting
(iii) Gap (iv) Browsing
Codes :
(A) (i) and (ii) are correct
(B) (ii) and (iii) are correct
(C) (i) and (iii) are correct
(D) (ii) and (iv) are correct

208. 'Kinesis' is related to
(A) communication (B) generation
(C) storage (D) none of these.

209. Arrange the following according to the year of establishments :
(i) NICNET (ii) INDONET
(iii) INFLIBNET (iv) MALIBNET

Codes :

(A) (iv), (i), (iii), (ii) (B) (iv), (ii), (i), (iii)

(C) (ii), (i), (iv), (iii) (D) (i), (iii), (iv), (ii)

210. Match the following :

	List – I		List – II
(a)	Library of Congress	(i)	1952
(b)	INSDOC	(ii)	1954
(c)	Delivery of Books Act	(iii)	1903
(d)	Imperial Library, Calcutta	(iv)	1800

Code :	(a)	(b)	(c)	(d)
(A)	(ii)	(i)	(iii)	(iv)
(B)	(i)	(iii)	(ii)	(iv)
(C)	(iv)	(i)	(ii)	(iii)
(D)	(i)	(ii)	(iii)	(iv)

211. IFLA Head office located at
   (A) Paris, France
   (B) Netherlands, in The Hague
   (C) Canada
   (D) London
212. .Library Association (LA) established in
   (A) 1876 (B) 1877
   (C) 1926 (D) 1923
213. International Federation of Library Associations and Institutions (IFLA) established in
   (A) 1909 (B) 1926
   (C) 1927 (D) 1949
214. American Library Association (ALA) established in
   (A) 1876 (B) 1877
   (C) 1926 (D) 1933
215. Special Library Association (SLA) US established in
   (A) 1909 (B) 1923
   (C) 1926 (D) 1933

216. Indian Library Association (ILA) established in

(A) 1924 (B) 1933

(C) 1949 (D) 1954

217. The Association of Information Management (ASLIB) established in

(A) 1924 (B) 1926

(C) 1927 (D) 1933

218. Indian Association of Special Libraries and Information Centers (IASLIC) established in

(A) 1933 (B) 1955

(C) 1977 (D) 2002

219. Commonwealth Library Association (COMLA) established in

(A) 1927 (B) 1972

(C) 1933 (D) 1955

220. Library Association LA (UK) changed its as CILIP in

(A) 2000 (B) 2001

(C) 2002 (D) 2003

221. Indian Association of Teachers of Library and Information Science (IATLIS) established in

(A) 1933 (B) 1955

(C) 1969 (D) 1972

222. Information about Indian research studies on bakery and milling is input to IFIS through

(A) The Central Rice Research Institute

(B) Indian Agricultural Research Institute

(C) National Institute of Nutrition

(D) Central Food Technological Research Institute

223. Match the following :

List 'A'	**List 'B'**
(1) Chattopadhyaya	(a) 1959 Committee Report
(2) Kothari Commission	(b) 1942 Report
(3) Sinha Committee Report	(c) 1986
(4) Fyzee Committee Report	(d) 1966

Codes :

(A) (c), (d), (a), (b) (B) (d), (c), (b), (a)
(C) (b), (d), (c), (a) (D) (d), (b), (a), (c)

224. UNESCO's information programme is known as
(A) NATIS (B) GIP
(C) UAP (D) UBC

225. in a communication model, noise refers to
(A) Loudness of signal
(B) lack of understanding between sender and receiver
(C) any disturbance which affects the transmission
(D) irrelevant information

226. Zero-growth libraries contradict the fifth law of library science. The statement is
(A) true, because no new books are added
(B) true, because the totla size of the bookstock is steady
(C) false, since the library may grow in other ways
(D) false, since there can be no zero-growth libraries

227. SENDOC is the national documentation centre for
(A) Science and Environment
(B) Sociology and Economics
(C) Sri Lanka
(D) Small Scale Enterprise

228. Library technology reports is a publication of ...
(A) ILA (B) ALA
(C) LA (D) IASLIC

229. The first ever library school was started by melvil dewey in USA in?

(A) 1887 (B) 1876

(C) 1875 (D) 1880

230. What is the essential aspect of information service?

(A) Retrieval of information

(B) Storage of information

(C) Collection of information

(D) Communication of information

231. What is the full form of ERNET?

(A) Engineering Network

(B) Eastern Regional Network

(C) Electronic Research Network

(D) Education and Research Network

232. WA Bordon. Initiated training in librarianship in India in?

(A) 1876 (B) 1877

(C) 1911 (D) 1923

233. The word Library is made of the word

(A) Liber (B) Libra

(C) Libre (C) Liberae

234. Which commission recommended 10% of the total college budget for development of libraries

(A) Dr. S. R. Rangnathan Committee

(B) Kothari Committee

(C) Mehrotra Committee

(D) Yash Pal

235. Listening to a lecture is

(A) information Listening

(B) evaluative listening

(C) emphatic Listening

(D) none of these

236. Teaching on TV is superior to class room instruction because
   (A) very large classes are made' possible and thus. it; is economically advantageous
   (B) experts for teaching a difficult topic can be arranged and others can be benefited from them
   (C) teaching materials can be filmed for reuse
   (D) All of these

237. Following are the experimental learning activities adopted by a teacher. Arrange them in cyclic order.
   (i) Accommodation (ii) Converging
   (iii) Assimilation (iv) Diverging

   Codes :
   (A) (i), (ii), (iii), (iv) (B) (iv), (iii), (ii), (i)
   (C) (ii), (iii), (iv), (i) (D) (iii), (i), (ii), (iv)

238. Listening is badly affected by
   (A) message overload-excess of listened material
   (B) high speed of speaking
   (C) a sizable hearing loss-physiological problem
   (D) all of the above

239. Which of the following skills has the largest share in communication time in schools/colleges?
   (A) Listening (B) Reading
   (C) Writing (D) Speaking

240. Which of the following teachers will you like most?
   (A) One who uses board occasionally
   (B) One who uses chart and maps
   (C) One who uses film projector along with the proper use of the board
   (D) One who uses motion picture as a last resort

241. The main purpose of evaluative listening is

(A) to accept or reject an idea given to the listener

(B) to evaluate the speaker's credibility and personality

(C) both of above

(D) none of these

242. CHEER stands for

(A) Children Enrichment Education Through Radio

(B) Child Health Education Electronic Recording

(C) Children for Engineers and Energy Requirement

(D) None of the above

243. The most important aspect of communication-listening, can be improved by

(A) making the attention fully paid

(B) making the communicated material novel-interesting and need based.

(C) making voice effective and impressive

(D) all of these

244. Educational TV was first introduced in India in the year

(A) 1961 (B) 1959

(C) 1968 (D) 1969

245. which of the following can not be a good way of communication in promoting literacy among villagers?

(A) Demonstration

(B) Reading and writing

(C) providing material on TV and film projector

(D) Large group discussion

246. SITE stands for

(A) System for International Technology and Engineering

(B) Satellite Instructional Television Experiment

(C) South Indian Trade Estate

(D) None of these

247. The process of communication enhances through:
    (A) belongingness
    (B) security and freedom to make choices
    (C) informality of meeting and avoidance of pressure
    (D) all of these
248. A student helps a teacher to solve the problem while the teacher was delivering the lecture. He was
    (A) an emphatic listener
    (B) an evaluative listener
    (C) a realistic listener
    (D) an informational listener
249. Which of the following is not a successful communicator?
    (A) One who presents material in a precise and clear way.
    (B) One who is able to adapt himself according to the language of the communicatee
    (C) One who knows a lot but is somewhat reserve in his attitude.
    (D) One who sometimes becomes informal before the receiver and develops rapport
250. As a chairman of UPSC while selecting a teacher you should, be
    (A) fair and impartial
    (B) able to judge the personality of candidates
    (C) encouraging to those appearing for interview.
    (D) All of these

Library Associations, Established Year and Headquarters

Sr. No.	*Title*	*Year*	*Place*
1	American Library Association	1876	Chicago
2	Library Association(uk)	1977	London
3	Special Library Association (SLA)US	1909	Washington
4	Indian Library Association (ILA)	1933	New Delhi
5	Indian Association of Special Libraries and Information Centers (IASLIC)	1955	Calcutta
6	International Federation of Library Associations (IFLA)	1927	The Hauge
7	Commonwealth Library Association (COMLA)	1972	Kingston
8	Association For Information Management (ASLIB)	1924	London
9	Indian Association of Teachers of Library and Information Sciences (IATLIS)	1969	India

ANSWERS

1 (B)	2 (C)	3 (A)	4 (A)	5 (B)	6 (C)
7 (A)	8 (C)	9 (A)	10 (B)	11 (B)	12 (C)
13 (B)	14 (A)	15 (D)	16 (C)	17 (D)	18 (B)
19 (A)	20 (D)	21 (A)	22 (D)	23 (B)	24 (D)
25 (B)	26 (B)	27 (C)	28 (D)	29 (D)	30 (B)
31 (B)	32 (A)	33 (A)	34 (A)	35 (B)	36 (D)
37 (B)	38 (D)	39 (B)	40 (C)	41 (B)	42 (C)
43 (A)	44 (B)	45 (B)	46 (D)	47 (D)	48 (B)
49 (A)	50 (D)	51 (B)	52 (C)	53 (C)	54 (B)
55 (B)	56 (B)	57 (A)	58 (D)	59 (A)	60 (A)
61 (C)	62 (C)	63 (D)	64 (D)	65 (B)	66 (D)
67 (C)	68 (A)	69 (D)	70 (D)	71 (A)	72 (B)

73 (B)	74 (D)	75 (A)	76 (B)	77 (C)	78 (D)
79 (D)	80 (A)	81 (D)	82 (D)	83 (D)	84 (C)
85 (A)	86 (A)	87 (C)	88 (A)	89 (D)	90 (A)
91 (B)	92 (A)	93 (D)	94 (B)	95 (D)	96 (B)
97 (C)	98 (B)	99 (C)	100 (A)	101 (C)	102 (C)
103 (C)	104 (A)	105 (B)	106 (A)	107 (C)	108 (A)
109 (B)	110 (A)	111 (D)	112 (C)	113 (C)	114 (D)
115 (C)	116 (A)	117 (C)	118 (A)	119 (A)	120 (B)
121 (D)	122 (A)	123 (C)	124 (C)	125 (B)	126 (B)
127 (C)	128 (A)	129 (B)	130 (B)	131 (B)	132 (D)
133 (B)	134 (B)	135 (D)	136 (C)	137 (B)	138 (A)
139 (D)	140 (A)	141 (A)	142 (B)	143 (C)	144 (D)
145 (C)	146 (C)	147 (C)	148 (A)	149 (B)	150 (B)
151 (D)	152 (C)	153 (A)	154 (B)	155 (B)	156 (C)
157 (A)	158 (B)	159 (A)	160 (B)	161 (D)	162 (D)
163 (B)	164 (A)	165 (A)	166 (A)	167 (D)	168 (A)
169 (D)	170 (C)	171 (D)	172 (C)	173 (C)	174 (D)
175 (A)	176 (D)	177 (C)	178 (A)	179 (B)	180 (D)
181 (A)	182 (B)	183 (A)	184 (C)	185 (A)	186 (B)
187 (A)	188 (B)	189 (B)	190 (B)	191 (D)	192 (B)
193 (A)	194 (D)	195 (C)	196 (D)	197 (C)	198 (D)
199 (A)	200 (A)	201 (B)	202 (A)	203 (D)	204 (A)
205 (B)	206 (C)	207 (C)	208 (A)	209 (D)	210 (C)
211 (B)	212 (B)	213 (C)	214 (A)	215 (A)	216 (B)
217 (A)	218 (B)	219 (B)	220 (C)	221 (C)	222 (D)
223 (A)	224 (C)	225 (B)	226 (A)	227 (D)	228 (B)
229 (A)	230 (D)	231 (D)	232 (C)	233 (B)	234 (B)
235 (A)	236 (D)	237 (B)	238 (D)	239 (A)	240 (C)
241 (C)	242 (A)	243 (D)	244 (A)	245 (B)	246 (B)
247 (D)	248 (A)	249 (C)	250 (D)		

2

Library Laws

PUBLIC LIBRARIES ACT IN INDIA

Since independence of India the following States have passed Public Libraries Acts

1. 1948 Tamilnadu
2. 1960 Andhra Pradesh
3. 1965 Karnataka
4. 1967 Maharashtra
5. 1979 West Bengal
6. 1988 Manipur
7. 1989 Haryana
8. 1989 Kerala
9. 1993 Mizoram
10. 1993 Goa
11. 2001 Odisha
12. 2000 Gujarat
13. 2005 Uttaranchal
14. 2006 Rajasthan
15. 2006 Uttar Pradesh
16. 2007 Lakshadweep
17. 2008 Bihar
18. 2009 Chattisgarh
19. 2009 Arunachal Pradesh

Other Important Laws

1. The Press and Registration of Books Act (1867)
2. Funds for the encouragement of literature (1898)
3. Imperial Library Act (1902)
4. Model Library Act (1930)
5. Delivery of Books (Public Libraries Act) 1954
6. Model Library Act / Bill (1963)

1. First Library Law is
   (A) Every Reader His/Her Book
   (B) Books are for use
   (C) Every Book its Reader
   (D) Library is a growing organism
2. Second Library Law is
   (A) Books are for use
   (B) Every Book its Reader
   (C) Library is a growing organism
   (D) Every Reader His/Her Book
3. Third Library Law is
   (A) Every Book its Reader
   (B) Books are for use
   (C) Library is a growing organism
   (D) Every Reader His/Her Book
4. Fifth Library Law is
   (A) Every Book its Reader
   (B) Books are for use
   (C) Library is a growing organism
   (D) Every Reader His/Her Book
5. Library Legislation refers to the development of
   (A) Academic Libraries (B) Special Libraries
   (C) Public Libraries (D) None of the above
6. which law of library Science relates to the growth of libraries
   (A) Forth law (B) First law
   (C) Second law (D) Fifth law
7. Books for all is the same according to which law of library Science
   (A) Books are for use
   (B) Every reader and his/her book
   (C) Every book and its reader
   (D) Save the time of the reader

8. There is no provision for Library cess in the Public Libraries act of:
   (A) West Bengal and Tamil Nadu
   (B) Andrapradesh and Maharashtra
   (C) Maharashtra and West Bengal
   (D) Gujrat and Tamilnadu
9. Extension services to the blind by a public library is justified by
   (A) the fourth law of library science
   (B) the fifth law of library science
   (C) he first law of library science
   (D) all the laws of library science
10. The Five laws of library science are a set of good norms to good practice in...
    (A) Society (B) Libraries
    (C) Librarianship (D) Library science
11. Arrange the following Laws of Library Science as given by Ranganathan:
    (i) Save the time of the reader
    (ii) Books are for use
    (iii) Every book has its reader
    (iv) Every Reader has his book
    Codes :
    (A) (ii), (iv), (iii), (i) (B) (iv), (ii), (i), (iii)
    (C) (ii), (i), (iv), (iii) (D) (iii), (ii), (i), (iv)
12. Arrange the following Public Library Acts according to their year of enactment:
    (i) Pondicherry (ii) Madras
    (iii) Haryana (iv) Orissa
    Codes :
    (A) (iv), (iii), (i), (ii) (B) (ii), (iii), (i), (iv)
    (C) (ii), (i), (iv), (iii) (D) (iii), (ii), (i), (iv)

13. **Assertion (A) :** A Library legislation provides proper governance and management.

Reason (R) : It ensures free public library service to all irrespective of caste, creed and sex.

Codes :

(A) Both (A) and (R) are true.

(B) Both (A) and (R) are false.

(C) (A) is true, but (R) is false.

(D) (A) is false, but (R) is true.

14. Arrange the following according to chronological order:

(i) Universal Copyright convention

(ii) Berne Convention

(iii) Indian Copyright Act

(iv) WIPO Copyright Act

Codes :

(A) (ii), (iv), (iii), (i) (B) (iii), (ii), (iv), (i)

(C) (i), (iii), (ii), (iv) (D) (ii), (i), (iii), (iv)

15. The Indian State which enacted the library legislation in the year 1948 is :

(A) Kerala

(B) Meghalaya

(C) Tamil Nadu (Madras)

(D) Rajasthan

16. Which law emphasizes the need for a reference service by the staffs?

(A) Every book its reader

(B) Books are for use

(C) Every reader his/her book

(D) Save the time of the reader

17. Where did Dr. S. R. Ranganathan put forth his five laws of library science?

(A) Meenakshi college, Annamalainagar
(B) Hindu College, New Delhi
(C) City College, Bangalore
(D) Christ College, Bangalore

18. Who gave the sixth law of library science "Every reader his/her freedom"?
(A) Walt Crawford (B) Michael Gorman
(C) James R. Rettig (D) Lenart Bjorneborn

19. Where is the headquarter of SLA?
(A) New York (B) Lagos
(C) Shimla (D) New Delhi

20. The five laws of Library Science published in the book form in the year
(A) 1924 (B) 1931
(C) 1928 (D) 1930

21. As per Indian Copyright Law, copyright is granted for
(A) Fifty years after the book is published
(B) Fifty years after the death of the author
(C) Sixty years after the book is published
(D) Sixty years after the death of the author

22. Which law strongly advocates user education programme in libraries:
(A) First Law (B) Second
(C) Third (D) Fourth

23. Which Law gives the message is that a library should be located at a central place where it is convenient to reach:
(A) Books are for Use
(B) Every reader his/her book
(C) Save the time of the reader
(D) The Library is a growing organism

24. Match the following :

	List - I	**List - II**
(a)	Library of Congress	(i) 1952
(b)	INSDOC	(ii) 1954
(c)	Delivery of Books Act	(iii) 1903
(d)	Imperial Library, Calcutta	(iv) 1800

Code :	**(a)**	**(b)**	**(c)**	**(d)**
(A)	(ii)	(i)	(iii)	(iv)
(B)	(i)	(iii)	(ii)	(iv)
(C)	(iv)	(i)	(ii)	(iii)
(D)	(i)	(ii)	(iii)	(iv)

25. The Delivery of Books (Public Libraries) Act, 1954 was not implemented in
    (A) Assam (B) Jammu and Kashmir
    (C) Haryana (D) Delhi

26. According to General Financial Rules, 2005, loss of how many volumes per thousand volumes issued / consulted in a year is to be taken as reasonable.
    (A) Three (B) Four
    (C) Five (D) Six

27. Delivery of Books (Public Libraries Act) enacted in
    (A) 1977 (B) 1944
    (C) 1967 (D) 1954

28. First library act was enacted in Great Britain in
    (A) 1847 (B) 1850
    (C) 1867 (D) 1840

29. The act enacted in India in 1856 on Intellectual Property Right was based on.
    (A) American Patent Law 1810
    (B) British Patent Law 1852
    (C) The Patent Bill
    (D) The Design Act of 1911

30. 'Fair use' is the norm for determining the legality of
    (A) Producing the second edition of a book
    (B) Photocopying an entire book
    (C) Making available a book to another library on inter-library loan
    (D) Prescribing a book as a text book.
31. Which Department of the government of India is deals with Public libraries
    (A) Department of Archeology
    (B) Department of Culture
    (C) Department of Higher Education
    (D) Department of Science and Technology
32. The also has certain responsibilities cast on him by the law
    (A) The Library is a growing organism
    (B) Books are for use
    (C) Every reader his/her book
    (D) Every book its reader
33. The Press and Registration of books Act was enacted in
    (A) 1847 (B) 1850
    (C) 1867 (D) 1840
34. The quotation "Where is the Wisdom, We Lost in Knowledge..." is by
    (A) John Keats (B) M. P. Carter
    (C) T. S. Eliot (D) Marshall McLuhan
35. First B.Lib. Science Course was introduced in
    (A) Aligarh Muslim University
    (B) University of Calcutta
    (C) University of Delhi
    (D) University of Madras

36. Universal Copyright conventions was in
    (A) 1949 (B) 1952
    (C) 1971 (D) 1931
37. The UNESCO Public Library Manifesto first issued in
    (A) 1949 (B) 1952
    (C) 1971 (D) 1931
38. Location of the Library Should be at a central place, which law strongly emphasis this statement
    (A) First Law (B) Second
    (C) Third (D) Fourth
39. Culcutta Public Library was opened to public on
    (A) 21st Mar 1836 (B) 21st Apr 1836
    (C) 21st May 1836 (D) 21st June 1836
40. The New Impirial Library of India Opened to public on
    (A) 3oth Jan 1903 (B) 3oth Jan 1901
    (C) 3oth Jan 1902 (D) 3oth Jun 1903
41. Who was the first librarian of Imperial Library of India
    (A) Lord Curzon (B) K.M. Asadulah
    (C) B. kesavan (D) John Macfarlane
42. Sadler Commission in India was setup in the year:
    (A) 1882 (B) 1902
    (C) 1917 (D) 1946
43. Model Public Library Bill in 1963 under the chairmanship was prepared
    (A) M.D.Sen (B) Venkatappaiah
    (C) S.R.Rangnathan (D) C.D.Deshmukh
44. What is Red Letter Day in the History of Britain
    (A) The Day British Library was setup
    (B) British Museum was established
    (C) British Library legislation became a reality
    (D) British Library Association formed

45. World's first library act was enacted in
    (A) India (B) UK
    (C) USA (D) Germany

46. Mudaliar commission in India was specially setup for the development of
    (A) Primary Education (B) Secondary Education
    (C) Higher Education (D) All of the above

47. in which of following state gets fund through library Cess
    (A) Tamil Nadu (B) Maharashtra
    (C) West Bengal (D) Manipur

48. When an author has not registered his/her work under copyright but legally proceeded over dispute of ownership. What is the validity of ownership?
    (A) No ownership without registration
    (B) It may not be legally tenable
    (C) Valid for 60 years
    (D) Both (a) and (b) are correct

49. Guide for the Preparation and Publication of Abstracts was published by
    (A) IFLA (B) FID
    (C) OCLC (D) UNESCO

50. The key factor that enforces uniformity throughout retrieval system is
    (A) Controlled vocabulary
    (B) Search strategy
    (C) User Profile
    (D) Database

51. By 2002, Which of the following states have enacted their respective Public Library Acts?
    (i) Haryana (ii) Uttar Pradesh
    (iii) Mizoram (iv) Rajasthan

Codes:

(A) (i) and (iii) are correct

(B) (i), (ii) and (iii) are correct

(C) (ii) and (iv) are correct

(D) (iii) and (iv) are correct

52. Arrange in sequence the following repository libraries according to their year of establishment

(a) Connemera Public Library, Chennai

(b) Delhi Public Library, Delhi

(c) Asiatic Society Library, Mumbai

(d) Central Reference Library, Kolkata

Codes :

(A) (d), (a), (c) and (b)

(B) (a), (b), (c) and (d)

(C) (b), (d), (a) and (c)

(D) (c), (a), (b) and (d)

53. The National Mission on Libraries, India was established in which year

(A) 2009 (B) 2010

(C) 2012 (D) 2011

54. Which Law states Library hours should be convenient to users?

(A) Fourth Law (B) Third Law

(C) Second Law (D) First Law

55. Public Library Law has already been passed in the following States. Identify the correct chronological order in which they were enacted.

(i) Uttaranchal (Uttarakhand)

(ii) Orissa

(iii) Gujarat

(iv) Haryana

Codes :

(A) (i) (ii) (iii) (iv) (B) (iv) (ii) (i) (iii)

(C) (ii) (iii) (iv) (i) (D) (iii) (ii) (i) (iv)

56. Match the following:

List-I (Library Act)	**List-II (Year of Enactment)**
(a) Orissa	(i) 2006
(b) Goa	(ii) 2005
(c) Uttaranchal	(iii) 2001
(d) Uttar Pradesh	(iv) 1994

Code :	**(a)**	**(b)**	**(c)**	**(d)**
(A)	(i)	(ii)	(iii)	(iv)
(B)	(iii)	(iv)	(ii)	(i)
(C)	(iv)	(iii)	(ii)	(i)
(D)	(ii)	(i)	(iii)	(iv)

57. Arrange the following according to their year of enactment:

(i) Tamil Nadu Public Library Act

(ii) Kerala Public Library Act

(iii) Maharashtra Public Library Act

(iv) Orissa Public Library Act

Codes :

(A) (i), (iii), (ii), (iv) (B) (ii), (iii), (iv), (i)

(C) (ii), (iii), (i), (iv) (D) (iv), (iii), (ii), (i)

58. The latest State, which enacted Public Libraries Act is:

(A) Arunachal Pradesh (B) Uttaranchal

(C) Uttar Pradesh (D) Orissa

59. By which law investment in unused books is a dead investment and a waste

(A) Second Law (B) Third Law

(C) First Law (D) Fourth Law

60. Amendment to 'Delivery of Books (Public Libraries) and Newspapers Act' was enacted in India in the year

(A) 1952 (B) 1954
(C) 1956 (D) 1962

61. Arrange in sequence the following state public Library Acts according to the rear of their enactment?
(a) West Bengal (b) Orisa
(c) Arunachal Pradesh (d) Karnataka
Codes:
(A) d, a, b, c (B) b, a, d, c
(C) c, b, d, a (D) d, b, c, a

62. Which law emphasises need for a library legislation?
(A) Fourth Law (B) Third Law
(C) Second Law (D) First Law

63. Goa Public Libraries Act
(A) 1991 (B) 1992
(C) 1993 (D) 1994

64. Tamil Nadu Public Libraries Act
(A) 1958 (B) 1947
(C) 1948 (D) 1949

65. Maharashtra Public Libraries Act
(A) 1966 (B) 1968
(C) 1967 (D) 1970

66. Andhra Pradesh Public Libraries Act
(A) 1958 (B) 1960
(C) 1962 (D) 1964

67. Kartnataka Public Libraries Act
(A) 1965 (B) 1945
(C) 1955 (D) 1975

68. West Bengal Public Libraries Act
(A) 1969 (B) 1979
(C) 1965 (D) 1978

69. Kerala Public Libraries Act
(A) 1969 (B) 1979
(C) 1989 (D) 1999

70. Haryana Public Libraries Act
    (A) 1986 (B) 1988
    (C) 1989 (D) 1990
71. Manipur Public Libraries Act
    (A) 1984 (B) 1986
    (C) 1988 (D) 1989
72. Mizoram Public Libraries Act
    (A) 1993 (B) 1991
    (C) 1992 (D) 1995
73. Orissa Public Libraries Act
    (A) 2000 (B) 2001
    (C) 2002 (D) 2005
74. Gujarat Public Libraries Act
    (A) 2001 (B) 2003
    (C) 2002 (D) 2005
75. Uttaranchal Public Libraries Act
    (A) 2005 (B) 2003
    (C) 2007 (D) 2009
76. Uttar Pradesh Public Libraries Act
    (A) 2004 (B) 2005
    (C) 2005 (D) 1989
77. Rajasthan Public Libraries Act
    (A) 2007 (B) 2008
    (C) 2004 (D) 2006
78. Bihar Public Libraries Act
    (A) 2006 (B) 2008
    (C) 2007 (D) 2009
79. Chattisgarh Public Libraries Act
    (A) 2002 (B) 2006
    (C) 2007 (D) 2008
80. Lakshadweep Public Libraries Act
    (A) 2005 (B) 2004
    (C) 2007 (D) 2008

81. Arunachal Pradesh Public Libraries Act
    (A) 2009 (B) 2010
    (C) 2008 (D) 2006
82. According to which law, children's libraries should be specially designed for children keeping in view the goal of the promotion of the use of books.
    (A) The library is a growing organism
    (B) Every reader his/her book
    (C) Save the time of the reader
    (D) Books are for use
83. Which law satisfy by Resource sharing and other cooperative programmes
    (A) Fifth Law (B) Fourth Law
    (C) Third Law (D) Second Law
84. Dr. S.R.R's Five Law of Library Science published in the book
    (A) Reference Service
    (B) Library Administration
    (C) Library Manual for School, College and Public Libraries
    (D) Five Laws of Library Science
85. Save the time of the reader is the
    (A) First Law (B) Second Law
    (C) Third Law (D) Fourth Law
86. When Imperial Library renamed by National Library
    (A) 1947 (B) 1948
    (C) 1950 (D) 1952
87. We know Five Laws of Library Science were enunciated by S.R.Ranganathan. At the time Where he worked?
    (A) as the Librarian of the University of Madras
    (B) as Professor in Banaras Hindu University
    (C) as Student at University College, London
    (D) as Director in DRTC

88. There are a few basic factors which may be applied in winning the hearts of the readers. They are
    (A) psychological factor, environmental factor, social factor
    (B) self factor, psychological factor, service factor
    (C) service factor, philosophical factor, self factor
    (D) technological factor, service factor, self factor.

89. Match the following :

List-I	List-II
(a) Maharashtra Public Libraries Act	(i) 2004
(b) Gujarat Public Libraries Act	(ii) 2005
(c) Orissa Public Libraries Act	(iii) 1967
(d) West Bengal Public Libraries Act	(iv) 1988
	(v) 1979

Code :	(a)	(b)	(c)	(d)
(A)	(i)	(iii)	(ii)	(iv)
(B)	(ii)	(v)	(iv)	(iii)
(C)	**(iii)**	**(i)**	**(ii)**	**(v)**
(D)	(v)	(ii)	(iv)	(iii)

90. Number of States in India which have enacted Public Library Legislation till date is
    (A) Seven (B) Ten
    (C) Thirteen (D) Nineteen

91. The first library Act in India was passed and implemented in
    (A) Maharashtra (B) Andhra Pradesh
    (C) Madras (D) Karnataka

92. The 'Five Laws of Library Science' propounded by Dr. S. R. Ranganathan, is which type of research ?
    (A) Applied research (B) Pure research
    (C) Basic research (D) Survey research.

93. 'Tree of porphyry' is formed as result of:

(A) Fusion (B) Potychotomy
(C) Dichotomy (D) Decachotomy

94. Who was Andrew Carnegie?
(A) Information Scientist
(B) Philanthropist
(C) Teacher in library science
(D) Librarian

95. Writing system was invented by:
(A) Ancient Egyptians (B) French
(C) Greek (D) Ancient Indians

96. The barriers to communication and information flow are:
(A) Language problem (B) Economic problem
(C) Political problem (D) All the above

97. Library Science is an art or Science:
(A) Science (B) Science & Art
(C) Art (D) None of these

98. today society consumes knowledge and information in:
(A) Developed society (B) Rich society
(C) Ablest society (D) All these

99. The model public library established in India with UNESCO's assistance was:
(A) National Library
(B) National. Science Library
(C) Connemara Public Library
(D) Delhi Public Library

100. The word reprography means reproduction of graphic materials, irrespective of whether they are hand written, typed printed and so on:
(a) True (b) False

101. Xerography is:
   (A) Diazographic process
   (B) Dry copying process
   (C) Wet copying process
   (D) None of the above

ANSWERS

1 (B)	2 (D)	3 (A)	4 (C)	5 (C)	6 (D)
7 (B)	8 (C)	9 (D)	10 (C)	11 (A)	12 (B)
13 (A)	14 (D)	15 (C)	16 (C)	17 (A)	18 (C)
19 (A)	20 (B)	21 (D)	22 (B)	23 (A)	24 (C)
25 (B)	26 (C)	27 (D)	28 (B)	29 (B)	30 (B)
31 (B)	32 (C)	33 (C)	34 (C)	35 (A)	36 (B)
37 (A)	38 (A)	39 (A)	40 (A)	41 (D)	42 (C)
43 (A)	44 (C)	45 (B)	46 (B)	47 (A)	48 (C)
49 (D)	50 (A)	51 (A)	52 (D)	53 (C)	54 (D)
55 (B)	56 (B)	57 (A)	58 (A)	59 (B)	60 (C)
61 (A)	62 (C)	63 (C)	64 (C)	65 (C)	66 (B)
67 (A)	68 (B)	69 (C)	70 (C)	71 (C)	72 (A)
73 (B)	74 (A)	75 (A)	76 (C)	77 (D)	78 (B)
79 (D)	80 (C)	81 (A)	82 (D)	83 (D)	84 (D)
85 (D)	86 (B)	87 (A)	88 (D)	89 (C)	90 (D)
91 (C)	92 (C)	93 (C)	94 (B)	95 (A)	96 (D)
97 (B)	98 (D)	99 (D)	100 (A)	101 (B)	

3
Types of Documents

1. What is the publication frequency of I.N.B?
   (A) Quarterly (B) Monthly
   (C) Weekly (D) Annual
2. World of learning Is a what source of information
   (A) Primary Source (B) Documentary Source
   (C) Secondary Source (D) Tertiary Source
3. Facts of File is a
   (A) Weekly list (B) Fortnightly
   (C) Monthly (D) Quarterly
4. What is the thesaurus?
   (A) A collection of selected terminology
   (B) Synonymous terms
   (C) List of words
   (D) All of the above
5. The tern lexicography is associated with:
   (A) Compilation of Encyclopedia
   (B) Compilation of Handbook
   (C) Compilation of Dictionaries
   (D) None of the above

6. A Pre-print is a/an
   (A) Article to be published
   (B) Conference Paper to be included in the proceedings
   (C) Neither (A) nor (B)
   (D) Both (A) and (B)
7. The study abroad is a/an
   (A) Encyclopedia (B) Year Book
   (C) Directory Handbook (D) Handbook
8. Which of the following is a tertiary source of Information?
   (A) Journal
   (B) Bibliography
   (C) Encyclopedia
   (D) Bibliography of Bibliography
9. Which one is E-Bibliographic database?
   (A) Nature (B) Blackwell
   (C) ISID (D) Springer
10. What is Intellectual Property?
   (A) Books
   (B) All reading material
   (C) Intellectual thoughts
   (D) All of the above
11. What type of information sources is most useful?
   (A) Reference sources
   (B) Non documentary sources
   (C) Documentary sources
   (D) Both (B) & (C)
12. Which of the following is the primary source of information?
   (A) Bibliography (B) Encyclopedia
   (C) Handwritten articles (D) Dictionary

13. VINITI is the national documentation centre of :
    (A) Poland (B) Slovakia
    (C) Hungary (D) Russia
14. digit of International Standard Book Number(ISBN) divided into
    (A) 2 parts (B) 3 parts
    (C) 4 parts (D) 5 parts
15. UAP stands for what of the following
    (A) United Academy of publication
    (B) Universal Association of Publishers
    (C) Universal Availability of Publications.
    (D) Universal Association of Publishers
16. In January 2005, International Standard Book Number (ISBN) consists of
    (A) 8 digits (B) 10 digits
    (C) 13 digits (D) 15 digits
17. What are the two parts of the annual report of the library
    (A) Primary and Secondary
    (B) Analytical and Systematic
    (C) Upper and Lower
    (D) Descriptive and Statistical
18. What is a Patent
    (A) An agreement to the Government
    (B) Document of the library
    (C) An agreement between the inventor and the Government
    (D) An agreement between library and Publisher
19. 'Informatics' is a term which was first used for documentation in
    (A) Britain (B) USA
    (C) USSR/Russia (D) India

20. Intellectual Property Rights are recognized by
    (A) Copyright (B) Patent
    (C) Both (D) Neither
21. Identify the primary document from the following:
    (A) Bibliography (B) Biography
    (C) Autobiography (D) None of the above
22. Identify the secondary source from the following:
    (A) Standards (B) Patents
    (C) Journals (D) Directories
23. MESH is the name of a
    (A) Medical (B) Library
    (C) C.S.I.R Unit (D) Controlled Vocabulary
24. Paul Otlet used the term 'Documentation' for the first time in a lecture at the International Congress at Brussels in
    (A) 1905 (B) 1920
    (C) 1931 (D) 1948
25. ISBN contains
    (A) 6 digits (B) 8 digits
    (C) 10 digits (D) 13 digits
26. 'Micropaedia' is in how many volumes?
    (A) 5 (B) 12
    (C) 15 (D) 20
27. 'Facts on File' is published from
    (A) India (B) Africa
    (C) U.S.A (D) Europe
28. 'Indian Science Abstract' is published by
    (A) INSDOC (B) ICSSR
    (C) DST (D) DRTC
29. If in the year 2000, a journal has reached its 40th volume, when was it first published
    (A) 1959 (B) 1960
    (C) 1961 (D) None of the above

30. The book 'Library Administration' was brought out by Ranganathan in
    (A) 1925 (B) 1933
    (C) 1931 (D) 1935
31. WIPO stands for:
    (A) World Information and Patents Organisation
    (B) World Intellectual Property Organisation
    (C) World International Property Organisation
    (D) World Information Protection Organisation
32. which of the following are produced by Institute of Scientific Information:
    (i) Science Citation Index
    (ii) Current Contents
    (iii) Index Medicus
    (iv) Atom Index

    Codes :
    (A) (i), (ii) and (iii) (B) (i) and (ii) only
    (C) (ii) and (iii) only (D) (i) and (iv) only
33. IPR stands for
    (A) Indian Press Registration
    (B) Intellectual Property Right
    (C) International Property Right
    (D) Indian Property Regulations.
34. 'Fair use' is the norm for determining the legality of
    (A) producing the second edition of a book
    (B) photocopying an entire book
    (C) making available a book to another library on inter-library loan
    (D) prescribing a book as a text book.

35. Match the following :

	List-I (Term)	List-II (Forms of Communication)
(a)	Invisible college	(i) Physical carrier
(b)	Noise	(ii) Formal channel
(c)	Medium	(iii) Barrier
(d)	Document	(iv) Informal channel

Code :	**(a)**	**(b)**	**(c)**	**(d)**
(A)	(i)	(ii)	(iii)	(iv)
(B)	(ii)	(i)	(iii)	(iv)
(C)	(iv)	(iii)	(ii)	(i)
(D)	(iv)	(iii)	(i)	(ii)

36. Identify the odd one :
   (A) LISA (B) Psychological Abstracts
   (C) Index Medicus (D) World of Learning

37. what is library literature?
   (A) Indexing journal
   (B) List of books of library science
   (C) Abstracting periodical
   (D) Directory of sources of library science

38. Match the following :

	List-I	List-II
(a)	Origin of a word	(i) World of Learning
(b)	Synonyms for a word	(ii) Dictionary of Etymology
(c)	How to install a gadget	(iii) Encyclopedia
(d)	Address of Oxford University	(iv) Manual
		(v) Thesaurus

Code :	**(a)**	**(b)**	**(c)**	**(d)**
(A)	(ii)	(v)	(iv)	(iii)
(B)	(v)	(iii)	(iv)	(i)
(C)	(v)	(iv)	(i)	(iii)
(D)	(ii)	(v)	(iv)	(i)

39. Which is the journal of Library and Information Science?
    (A) Abacus
    (B) Actanumerica
    (C) Interlending and Document supply
    (D) All the above

40. Library technology reports is a publication of ...
    (A) ILA (B) ALA
    (C) LA (D) IASLIC

41. Which one is Library and Information Science Journal name?
    (A) Reference Reviews incorporating ASLIB Book Guide
    (B) Reference Reviews incorporating ASLIB Book journals
    (C) Reference Reviews incorporating ASLIB Book Review
    (D) Reference Reviews incorporating ASLIB E-Book

42. "It is a library with little or no physical presence of books, periodicals, reading space or support staff, but are that disseminate disseminate selective information directly to distribute library customers, usually electronically". Said by whom?
    (A) Kay Gapen (B) Powell
    (C) Sherwell (D) H. G. Wells

43. The concept of concretes and processes was given by.
    (A) Kaiser (B) H. P. Luhn
    (C) Derek Austin (D) S. R. Ranganathan

44. "A library is a public institution or establishment charged with the care of collection of books, the duty of making them accessible to those who require the use of them and the task of converting every person in its neighborhood into a habitual library goers and reader of books."Quoted by whom?

    (A) Dr S R Ranganathan (B) K.N.Raj
    (C) C.A.Cutter (D) W.C.Sayers

45. An entry that is made for the subject of a chapter in a book is referred to as

    (A) Cross Refernece Entry
    (B) Cross Reference Index Entry
    (C) Class Index Entry
    (D) Book Index Entry

46. Who suggested for Book Order Vigilance Pad (BOVP)?

    (A) C. A. Cutter (B) Melvil Dewey
    (C) Michael Gorman (D) S. R. Ranganathan.

47. In Sears, List of Subject Headings preferred headings are indicated by

    (A) Marking them as preferred headings
    (B) Printing them in bold type
    (C) Underlining them
    (D) Italicising them

48. Content in a Reference sources are arranged in

    (A) Chronological (B) Alphabetical
    (C) Both (D) None of the above

49. Lexicon refers to

    (A) Bibliography (B) Dictionary
    (C) Encyclopaedia (D) Directory

50. The term 'Thesaurus' is associated with

    (A) Directory (B) Bibliography
    (C) Dictionary (D) None of the above

51. Which of the following is not a secondary source of information
    (A) An encyclopedia
    (B) A textbook
    (C) A biographical dictionary
    (D) Patents
52. Which of the following reference source will you consult to locate information on the Pokharn test?
    (A) Encyclopedia of Britannica
    (B) Asian Recorder
    (C) Commonwealth Universities Yearbook
    (D) Dictionary of National Biography
53. Can a book have both ISBN & ISSN?
    (A) Yes (B) No
54. The following is not an example of re-packaging of information
    (A) Trend report (B) Catalogue
    (C) Summary (D) Digest
55. A book published as ebook, paperback, Hard cover. How ISBN will be assigned?
    (A) All editions have same ISBN
    (B) All editions have different ISBN
    (C) [E-book],[PBK, HBK]
    (D) All the above
56. ISBN changed from 10 digits to 13 from
    (A) January, 2007 (B) January, 2008
    (C) January, 2006 (D) January, 2005
57. Which publication was not authored by S.R. Ranaganathan?
    (A) Prolegomena to libraryclassification
    (B) Reference Service
    (C) Ramanujan : The man and the Mathematician
    (D) Living with Books

58. The Ten digit ISBN format was developed by
    (A) ISO (B) Bowker
    (C) World Scientific (D) Scribner

59. 'Five Laws of Library Science' was first published in
    (A) 1925 (B) 1930
    (C) 1931 (D) 1933

60. **Assertion (A) :** Primary source is one in which information is original.

    Reason (R) : Secondary sources repack the original information.

    (A) Both (A) and (R) are true.
    (B) (A) is true but (R) is false.
    (C) (A) is false but (R) is true.
    (D) Both (A) and (R) are false.

61. Arrange the following according to their development:
    (I) CCC (II) ISBD
    (III) CCF (IV) MARC II

    Codes :

    (A) (I), (IV), (II), (III) (B) (I), (II), (IV), (III)
    (C) (I), (IV), (III), (II) (D) (IV), (II), (III), (I)

62. Which one is not a Canon (as given by Ranganthan)?
    (A) Canon of Comprehensiveness
    (B) Canon of Consistence
    (C) Canon of Context
    (D) Canon of Currency

63. 'Half-life' in Information Science relates to
    (A) Rate of obsolescence (B) Rate of growth
    (C) Degree of scatter (D) Information explosion

64. Which library is authorized to receive books under 'Delivery of Books Act'?

(A) National Science Library, Delhi
(B) Central Library, Delhi
(C) State Central Library, Mumbai
(D) Parliament Library, Delhi

65. The term 'Exponential growth' refers to
(A) Linear growth
(B) Normal mode of distribution
(C) Geometric Progression
(D) Arithmetic Progression

66. "Publishers' Weekly" is published by
(A) H. W. Wilson, New York
(B) R. R. Bowker, London
(C) American Library Association, Chicago
(D) Aslib, London

67. **Assertion (A) :** Collection development must be done judiciously.
Reason (R) : Demand is the only governing factor in book selection. Codes :
(A) (A) is true and (R) is false.
(B) Both (A) and (R) are true and (R) is the correct explanation of (A).
(C) (A) is false and (R) is true.
(D) Both (A) and (R) are true, but (R) is not a correct explanation of (A).

68. **Assertion (A) :** LISA is a primary source of information.
Reason (R) : All primary sources provide original information. Codes :
(A) (A) is false, but (R) is true.
(B) (A) is true, but (R) is false.
(C) Both (A) and (R) are false.
(D) Both (A) and (R) are true.

69. **Assertion (A) :** According to the fifth Law of Library Science, Library is a growing organization.

Reason (R) : All resources of library are supposed to grow. Codes :

(A) (A) is true, but (R) is false.
(B) (A) is false, but (R) is true.
(C) Both (A) and (R) are false.
(D) Both (A) and (R) are true.

70. Arrange the following Laws of Library Science as given by Ranganathan :
(i) Save the time of the reader
(ii) Books are for use
(iii) Every book has its reader
(iv) Every Reader has his book

Codes :

(A) (ii), (iv), (iii), (i) (B) (iv), (ii), (i), (iii)
(C) (ii), (i), (iv), (iii) (D) (iii), (ii), (i), (iv)

71. Arrange the following in chronological order:
(i) ISBD
(ii) MARC
(iii) CCF
(iv) Resource Description and Access (RDA)

Codes :

(A) (ii), (i), (iii), (iv) (B) (i), (iv), (iii), (ii)
(C) (iii), (iv), (i), (ii) (D) (ii), (iv), (i), (iii)

72. Match the following

	List - I	List - II
(a)	Books in Print	(i) Directory
(b)	World of Learning	(ii) Trade bibliography
(c)	Keesing's Record of World Events	(iii) Travel guide
(d)	Fodor's Guide to India	(iv) Newspaper digest

Code :	**(a)**	**(b)**	**(c)**	**(d)**
(A)	(ii)	(i)	(iv)	(iii)
(B)	(ii)	(iii)	(i)	(iv)
(C)	(iv)	(i)	(ii)	(iii)
(D)	(iii)	(ii)	(i)	(iv)

73. Official Publications (Govt) belongs to which sources
    (A) Primary sources (B) Secondary sources
    (C) Tertiary Sources (D) None of the above

74. ISBN consists of
    (A) 6 digits (B) 8 digits
    (C) 13 digits (D) 15 digits

75. **Assertion (A) :** Indexing periodical retrieves information, which includes brief summary of the article.
    Reason (R) : It provides list of articles along with the title, authors and other bibliographic details.
    Codes :
    (A) Both (A) and (R) are true.
    (B) Both (A) and (R) are false.
    (C) (A)is true, but (R) is false.
    (D) (A) is false, but (R) are true

76. Arrange the following in the chronological sequence of their development.
    (i) ISBD (ii) CCF
    (iii) FRBR (iv) MARC
    Codes :
    (A) (i), (ii), (iv), (iii) (B) (iv), (i), (ii), (iii)
    (C) (iii), (ii), (iv), (i) (D) (i), (iv), (ii), (iii)

77. Library Literature is a
    (A) Primary source of information
    (B) Secondary source of information
    (C) Tertiary source of information
    (D) Literary source of information

78. The frequency of Data India is
(A) Weekly (B) Fortnightly
(C) Monthly (D) Bi-monthly

79. BERNE CONVENTION is concerned with
(A) Translations (B) Copyright
(C) Patents (D) Standards

80. Fair use' is a term most relevant to
(A) Intellectual Property Rights
(B) Books borrowed for home reading
(C) Copy right
(D) Use of reference books

81. In 1967, ISBN generated based upon Standard Book Numbering (SBN), Who created SBN?
(A) Gordon Foster (B) David Whittaker
(C) WH Smith (D) Emery Koltay

82. Whether intellectual property can be sold.
(A) No (B) Sale is possible
(C) Yes (D) None of these

83. When was the International institute of Documentation established?
(A) 1931 (B) 1934
(C) 1940 (D) 1945

84. in which year the ISBN allocation office in India shifted from Kolkatta to Delhi?
(A) 2009 (B) 2010
(C) 2011 (D) 2012

85. In which year International institute of Documentation changed to International federation of Documentation?
(A) 1931 (B) 1937
(C) 1945 (D) 1948

86. Who published the journal International classification?
(A) IFLA (B) UNESCO
(C) ISKO (D) ALA

87. Which is/are not the part of ISBN

1. Group identifier	2. Country identifier
3. Publisher identifier	4. Title identifier
5. Check digit	6. 978

Codes :

(A) 1 & 2 only (B) 2 & 6 only
(C) 6 only (D) None of the above

88. Library Techology Report is a publication of
(A) ALA (B) IASLIC
(C) LA (D) ILA

89. ABGILA is a quarterly publication of
(A) Assam Library Association
(B) Andhra Desa Library Association
(C) Indian Library Association
(D) Raja Ram Mohun Roy Foundation

90. Encyclopedia of library and Information Science is published by
(A) H. W. Wilson (B) R. R. Bowker
(C) Marcel Dekker (D) Andrew Deutsch

91. The secondary source of information comprised of:
(A) Text books and research monographs.
(B) Subject periodicals and encycyclopaedias
(C) Indexing and Abstracting periodicals
(D) Bibliography and patents

92. Who categorized information source into conventional, non conventional, neo conventional and micro documents :
(A) Ranganthan (B) Bradford
(C) Grogan (D) Henson

93. Article published in research journal are…
(A) Reference sources (B) Secondary sources
(C) Primary sources (D) Tertiary sources

94. Patents belongs to which sources
    (A) Primary Sources (B) Secondary Sources
    (C) Tertiary Sources (D) None of the above
95. Standards belongs to which sources
    (A) Primary sources (B) Secondary sources
    (C) Tertiary Sources (D) None of the above
96. world of learning is a what source of information
    (A) Primary source (B) Documentary source
    (C) Secondary source (D) Tertiary source
97. Indian books in Print are published from
    (A) Tamil nadu (B) Chennai
    (C) Bombay (D) New Delhi
98. Cumulative book index is published from
    (A) India (B) USA
    (C) Canada (D) Thailand
99. Statesman year book is published from
    (A) London (B) New york
    (C) Calcutta (D) Chicago
100. who is the editor of "Library Herald"
    (A) Krishan Kumar (B) C. K. Sharma
    (C) S. R. Ranganathan (D) F.Monbray Volte
101. Facts of File is weekly digest of
    (A) Indian events (B) American events
    (C) World events (D) England events
102. Who is the first editor of "Modern Librarian"?
    (A) F.Monbrary Volte (B) Dr. S. R. Ranganathan
    (C) J. D. Brown (D) Krishan Kumar
103. Indian national Bibliographical first appeared in
    (A) 1947 (B) 1957
    (C) 1967 (D) 1937
104. Who is the author of "Dictionary of anonymous and pseudonymous literature"

(A) S. Halkett & J. Laing (B) Robert Proctor
(C) Ralph De sols (D) Hanuman Sastri

105. Compton year book contains
(A) Political events (B) Cultural events
(C) Outstanding events (D) Economic events

106. Online Europa year book has a coverage since
(A) 1965 (B) 1975
(C) 1984 (D) 1985

107. Research periodicals are which category of sources?
(A) Primary (B) Secondary
(C) Tertiary (D) Non documentary

108. Reference sources are those
(A) Which are large in size?
(B) Which are read at home easily?
(C) Which used to obtain particular information?
(D) Which are costly?

109. Who is the publisher of Encyclopedia of Library and information science?
(A) Boweker (B) H.W.Wilson company
(C) M.Dekker (D) H.W.Wilson

110. which part of new encyclopedia Britannica is useful for ready references?
(A) Macropaedia (B) Propaedia
(C) Micropaedia (D) Premedia

111. Year book are also known as
(A) Hand book (B) Annual
(C) Directory (D) Dictionary

112. what is India: A reference annual?
(A) Year Book (B) Almonac
(C) Gide book (D) Hand book

113. what is Trade bibliography?

(A) List of Author Bibliography
(B) List of Special Bibliography
(C) List of books in print or for sale compiled by a publisher
(D) List of books of trade Library

114. who publishes INIS Atom Index?
(A) INIS (Viena) (B) LC
(C) ICSU (D) AGRIS

115. What is the meaning of E-Documents?
(A) All Documents other than printed
(B) Non-Paper documents
(C) In electronic form such as Cassettes, CD-ROMs, etc.
(D) Audio visual tools

116. which of the following is not the documents?
(A) Manuscript (B) Book
(C) Inscription (D) Periodical

117. Dictionaries belongs to which sources
(A) Primary Sources (B) Secondary Sources
(C) Tertiary Sources (D) None of the above

118. What are non- documentary sources?
(A) Which are in printed form.
(B) Which are in not printed form
(C) Which are nor documents
(D) None of these

119. Today which type of information sources is most useful?
(A) Reference sources
(B) Documentary source
(C) Non- Documentary source
(D) Both the Documentary and Non-Documentary sources

120. What do you call a collection of maps, tables, charts, etc?
(A) Globe (B) Gazetteer
(C) Atlas (D) Map

121. Monographs belongs to which sources?
(A) Primary Sources (B) Secondary Sources
(C) Tertiary Sources (D) Non of the above

122. Encyclopedia Americana consists of
(A) 20 Volumes (B) 25 Volumes
(C) 28 Volumes (D) 30 Volumes

123. which of the following are not the secondary sources?
(A) Encyclopedia (B) Digest
(C) Thesis (D) Text book

124. what is the publication frequency of books in print?
(A) Monthly (B) Weekly
(C) Annually (D) Quarterly

125. What is National bibliography?
(A) List of books of National Library
(B) List of books published in a particular Nation
(C) List of books written by National government
(D) List of books on a nation

126. what is world of learning?
(A) Directory (B) Encyclopedia
(C) Dictionary (D) Year book

127. What is the frequency of I.N.B.?
(A) Quarterly (B) Monthly
(C) Weekly Page (D) Annual

128. 'Facts on File' is a
(A) Weekly list (B) Fortnightly
(C) Monthly (D) Quarterly

129. MESH is a
(A) Thesaurus (B) Dictionary
(C) Journal (D) Library

130. ISBN now consists of how many digit
    (A) 10 (B) 9
    (C) 15 (D) 13
131. How many digits have in the ISSN
    (A) 10 (B) 8
    (C) 13 (D) 15
132. Financial support given to libraries are of two types - Recurring and
    (A) Ad-hoc (B) Endowments
    (C) Annual (D) Non-recurring
133. Principle of maximum aggregate benefit is concerned with__
    (A) Growth of library (B) Library use
    (C) Library service (D) Library fee
134. .... takes items of expenditure for libraries as the working data for allocation of funds.
    (A) Method of details (B) Per capita method
    (C) Principle of economy (D) Library budget
135. A budget which mainly covers items of current revenue and expenditure is called __.
    (A) Programme budget (B) Welfare economics
    (C) Current budgeting (D) Capital budgeting
136. The library budget of a university is passed by the?
    (A) Senate (B) Executive Council
    (C) Academic Council (D) Research Council
137. In fund accounting, _______ fund can not be used for other purposes.
    (A) Recurring (B) Non-recurring
    (C) Restricted (D) Encumbering
138. Scrutiny of financial transactions is called
    (A) Budgeting (B) Programming
    (C) Accounting (D) Auditing

139. Bibliographies belongs to which sources
    (A) Primary sources (B) Secondary sources
    (C) Tertiary Sources (D) None of the above
140. When was Browne charging system started?
    (A) 1895 (B) 1896
    (C) 1899 (D) 1875
141. Who started Newyork Charging system?
    (A) Peter Drucker (B) Elton Mayo
    (C) John Cotton Dana (D) Francis Bacon
142. When did electrically operated book charging system introduced first?
    (A) 1926 (B) 1905
    (C) 1933 (D) 1932
143. How m any columns are there in the accession register?
    (A) 10 (B) 12
    (C) 14 (D) 16
144. What are the standard size of the Accession Register is
    (A) 16" * 12" (B) 16" * 13"
    (C) 16" * 11" (D) 16" * 18"
145. ________ is a legal document and can be used as a source of industrial information.
    (A) Report (B) Law Review
    (C) Patent (D) Specification
146. In Encyclopaedia Britannica, ___________ acts as an index to macropaedia.
    (A) Bibliography (B) Introduction Part
    (C) Propaedia (D) Micropaedia
147. One of the book selection principles states that "the best reading for the largest number at the .... Cost."
    (A) maximum (B) medium
    (C) least (D) zero

148. Payments for the books purchased can be made only after
    (A) accessioning
    (B) classification
    (C) Cataloguing
    (C) arrangement in the shelve

149. The standard size of an accession register is?
    (A) 15" x 13"   (B) 16 x 13"
    (C) 12" x 5"   (D) 5" x 3"

150. ISBN stands for ________
    (A) Integrated Services Bibliographic Network
    (B) Indian Standard Book Number
    (C) International Standard Book Number
    (D) International Standard for Book and Non- book

151. PRECIS was developed by Derek Austin for use in the
    (A) BNB   (B) INB
    (C) ISBD   (D) ISBN

152. Books misplaced on the shelves by readers are restored. This work is referred to as.
    (A) Shelving   (B) Stock verification
    (C) Shelf rectification   (D) Shifting

153. Outdated and seldom used books are withdrawn from the library is known as.
    (A) Shelving   (B) Weeding
    (C) Circulating   (D) Guiding

154. The objective of library binding is ________ of the library materials.
    (A) Proper organisation   (B) **accessibility.**
    (C) durability   (D) humidity control

155. All part and pages of a volume are correctly sequenced in the first stage of binding process known as?
    (A) sewing   (B) guard
    (C) pulling   (D) collation

156. Sheets before and after the text of a book are called ________. .

(A) End papers (B) Attach cover
(C) Head bands (D) Gilding

157. Leather being used as one of the binding materials i.e., ________ is the strongest leather.

(A) Roan (B) Imitation
(C) Pig skin (D) Sheep skin

158. ________ has prescribed certain standards for library binding.

(A) ILA (B) ALA
(C) BLA (D) NBT

159. Which of the following is a Secondary source of information?

(A) Journal
(B) Text book
(C) Bibliography of Bibliography
(D) Bibliography

160. Berne Convention and Universal Copyright Convention was revised in Paris in

(A) 1949 (B) 1952
(C) 1971 (D) 1931

161. C. W. Hanson

(A) Categorized information need into current approach, everyday approach, and exhaustive approach.
(B) Divides documentary sources of information into primary and secondary.
(C) Divides documentary sources of information into primary, secondary and tertiary.
(D) Classified documentary sources of information into Conventional, Neo Conventional, Non Conventional and meta document.

162. Denis Grogan
    (A) Categorized information need into current approach, everyday approach, and exhaustive approach.
    (B) Divides documentary sources of information into primary and secondary.
    (C) Divides documentary sources of information into primary, secondary and tertiary.
    (D) Classified documentary sources of information into Conventional, Neo Conventional, Non Conventional and meta document.
163. Which of the following is a Tertiary Sources of Information?
    (A) Journal
    (B) Bibliography
    (C) Encyclopaedia
    (D) Bibliography of Bibliographies
164. The Press and Registration of books Act was enacted in
    (A) 1847 (B) 1850
    (C) 1867 (D) 1840
165. Dr. S. R. Ranganathan
    (A) Categorized information need into current approach, everyday approach, and exhaustive approach.
    (B) Divides documentary sources of information into primary and secondary.
    (C) Divides documentary sources of information into primary, secondary and tertiary.
    (D) Classified documentary sources of information into Conventional, Neo Conventional, Non Conventional and meta document.
166. Granthana is an official publication of

(A) ILA (B) IASLIC
(C) RRRLF (D) APLA

167. Emerald full text Database is published from
(A) USA (B) Germany
(C) France (D) U.K.

168. which national agency in India is assigning the ISBN?
(A) Raja Ram Mohan Roy National Education Resource Centre
(B) Delhi Public Library
(C) Federation of Publishers in India
(D) National Library of India

169. Libraries as Gateways to Knowledge is the title of the document of
(A) National Information Policy, 1986
(B) Information Technology Act, 2000
(C) National Knowledge Commission on Libraries, 2007
(D) None of the above

170. Guides to Libraries belongs to which sources
(A) Primary sources (B) Secondary sources
(C) Tertiary Sources (D) None of the above

171. JSTOR is an online system for archiving and accessing academic journals. It is located in
(A) Germany (B) UK
(C) USA (D) Budapest

172. where is the head quarter of Patent Information System in India?
(A) Pune (B) Mumbai
(C) Nagpur (D) Delhi

173. Review of progress belongs to which sources
(A) Primary sources (B) Secondary sources
(C) Tertiary Sources (D) None of the above

174. List of research in progress belongs to which sources
   (A) Primary sources (B) Secondary sources
   (C) Tertiary Sources (D) None of the above
175. ISSN allotted for
   (A) E-Book (B) Book
   (C) Bond Volumes (D) Jorunal
176. Who introduced Three card system
   (A) Krishan Kumar (B) C. K. Sharma
   (C) Cutter (D) S. R. Ranganathan
177. CCF stands for
   (A) Common Communication Format
   (B) Centre for Communication Format
   (C) Committee for Communication Format
   (D) Common Curriculum Format
178. who publishes Annals of Library Science and documentation?
   (A) ILA (B) INSDOC
   (C) DRTC (D) IASLIC
179. What one is full text e-Resource?
   (A) JCCC
   (B) ISID
   (C) Science finder scholar
   (D) ACS
180. Directories belongs to which sources
   (A) Primary Sources (B) Secondary Sources
   (C) Tertiary Sources (D) None of the above
181. The Electronic Library is....................
   (A) A Magazine (B) A Journal Name
   (C) A Library (D) An Encyclopeadia
182. what is APS?
   (A) A Search Engine?
   (B) A Full-text e-resourse

(C) Bibliographic database
(D) Library Management Software

183. Conference proceedings are considered as .... documents.
(A) Conventional (B) Primary
(C) Secondary (D) Tertiary

184. IFLA took up the "Universal Availability of Publication" program in the year.
(A) 1973 (B) 1976
(C) 1972 (D) 1970

185. Currently "Science Citation Index" is published by.
(A) Emerald (B) Springer
(C) Thomson (D) Elsevier

186. Library Technology Report is a publication of
(A) ALA (B) IASLIC
(C) LA (D) ILA

187. Generally the information sources are divided mainly in to following categories?
(A) Primary and secondary.
(B) Reference and information sources.
(C) Documentary and non-documentary
(D) Books and periodicals

188. How many volumes Micropaedia of new Encyclopedia Britannica is published?
(A) 2 (B) 10
(C) 11 (D) 12

189. Arrange the following elements of ISBN in proper order
(a) Check Digit
(b) Registration Group Element
(c) Publication Element
(d) Registration Element

Option :

(A) (a), (c), (b), (d) (B) (c), (a), (d), (b)

(C) (d), (b), (a), (c) (D) (b), (d), (c), (a)

190. Which one is the most important problem being faced by Institutional Repositories for archiving the documents ?

(A) Availability (B) Rarity

(C) Copyright issues (D) Author's resistance

191. Word of learning is Published by

(A) Asian events (B) Keesing's

(C) Europa publication (D) Harper & Row

192. Who was Published the monthly Journal "The Library World'

(A) Krishan kumar (B) J. D. Brown

(C) H. W. Wilson (D) K. Navlavi

193. The Indian National Bibliography does not include

(A) Books published in India in English

(B) Official reports

(C) Books on India, published abroad

(D) Books published in recognized Indian languages

194. New Encyclopaedia Britannica is published from

(A) London (B) New York

(C) Paris (D) Chicago

195. Indian Journal of Chemistry "A" is published by

(A) NISCAIR

(B) Indian Science Academy

(C) ILA

(D) IFLA

196. RRLF provides the?

(A) ISSN (B) ISBN

(C) CCF (D) MARC

ANSWERS

1 (B)	2 (C)	3 (A)	4 (D)	5 (C)	6 (D)
7 (D)	8 (D)	9 (C)	10 (D)	11 (D)	12 (C)
13 (D)	14 (C)	15 (C)	16 (B)	17 (D)	18 (C)
19 (D)	20 (C)	21 (B)	22 (D)	23 (D)	24 (A)
25 (D)	26 (B)	27 (D)	28 (A)	29 (C)	30 (D)
31 (B)	32 (B)	33 (B)	34 (B)	35 (C)	36 (D)
37 (D)	38 (D)	39 (C)	40 (B)	41 (A)	42 (B)
43 (A)	44 (A)	45 (D)	46 (C)	47 (B)	48 (C)
49 (B)	50 (C)	51 (D)	52 (B)	53 (A)	54 (C)
55 (B)	56 (A)	57 (D)	58 (A)	59 (C)	60 (A)
61 (A)	62 (A)	63 (A)	64 (B)	65 (D)	66 (B)
67 (B)	68 (A)	69 (D)	70 (A)	71 (A)	72 (A)
73 (A)	74 (C)	75 (A)	76 (B)	77 (C)	78 (A)
79 (B)	80 (C)	81 (A)	82 (C)	83 (A)	84 (C)
85 (B)	86 (C)	87 (D)	88 (A)	89 (C)	90 (C)
91 (C)	92 (A)	93 (C)	94 (A)	95 (A)	96 (C)
97 (D)	98 (B)	99 (A)	100 (A)	101 (C)	102 (A)
103 (B)	104 (A)	105 (C)	106 (D)	107 (A)	108 (C)
109 (C)	110 (B)	111 (B)	112 (A)	113 (C)	114 (A)
115 (C)	116 (C)	117 (B)	118 (B)	119 (C)	120 (C)
121 (A)	122 (D)	123 (C)	124 (C)	125 (B)	126 (A)
127 (B)	128 (A)	129 (A)	130 (D)	131 (B)	132 (B)
133 (C)	134 (D)	135 (D)	136 (B)	137 (A)	138 (D)
139 (C)	140 (A)	141 (C)	142 (D)	143 (C)	144 (B)
145 (C)	146 (D)	147 (C)	148 (A)	149 (B)	150 (C)
151 (A)	152 (C)	153 (B)	154 (C)	155 (D)	156 (A)
157 (D)	158 (B)	159 (B)	160 (C)	161 (B)	162 (C)
163 (D)	164 (C)	165 (D)	166 (C)	167 (D)	168 (A)
169 (C)	170 (C)	171 (C)	172 (C)	173 (B)	174 (C)
175 (D)	176 (D)	177 (A)	178 (B)	179 (D)	180 (C)
181 (B)	182 (B)	183 (B)	184 (C)	185 (C)	186 (A)
187 (C)	188 (C)	189 (D)	190 (C)	191 (C)	192 (B)
193 (B)	194 (D)	195 (A)	196 (B)		

4

Reference Services

1. The term 'bibliometrics' was first used by
   (A) S. R. Ranganathan (B) Alan Pritchard
   (C) Allen Kent (D) A. C. Foskett
2. Indexing and abstracting sources are available in print, optical and online. Among the three formats there is usually
   (A) a difference in price, but not capability
   (B) no difference in price, but difference in capability
   (C) a difference both in price and in capability
   (D) no difference in price or capability
3. The subject headings "Money" and "Inflation" are both used in a retrieval system
   (A) be linked by a "see also" reference
   (B) be linked by a "see" reference
   (C) be linked by both "see" and "see also" references
   (D) not be linked
4. Generally a reference service of a library in the conventional form is processed through the stages which are

(A) preparation, service, assimilation
(B) indexing, orientation, delivery of the query's reply
(C) orientation, user's study, photocopy supplied
(D) preparation, orientation, delivery of the query's reply.

5. Evaluatiion criteria for maps and atlases includes
(a) scale and size
(b) projection
(c) location key,grid system
(d) topography, the use of colours

Codes:

(A) (a), (b) and (c) (B) (a), (b) and (d)
(C) (b), (c) and (d) (D) All of the above

6. A bibliography is a systematic list of documents prepared for a particular purpose on the basis of some criteria. These criteria may be
(i) documents on a subject,
(ii) of a country or
(iii) of the whole of available knowledge

Codes:

(A) i & ii (B) i & iii
(C) ii & iii (D) i, ii, iii

7. Abstracting service provides...
(A) Abstract of articles
(B) Whole bibliographic description of articles
(C) Whole bibliographic description along with abstracts of article
(D) Whole bibliographic sources

8. What is Bibliometry?
(A) Function of Library Network
(B) Information Management Service
(C) Information Management Tool
(D) Library Service

9. The term "Information Service" is an improvised name ...
   (A) Administration (B) Documentation
   (C) Bibliography (D) Reference service
10. dentify the branches of bibliography from the list?
    1. Analytical or critical
    2. Systematic or enumerative
    3. Descriptive
    4. Historical
    5. Textual

    Codes:
    (A) 1, 3, 4, 5 (B) 2, 3, 4, 5
    (C) 1, 4, 5 (D) 1, 2, 3, 4, 5
11. Citation indexing was first developed in the field of
    (A) Science (B) Mathematics
    (C) Law (D) Social sciences
12. BNB is published
    (A) Weekly (B) Monthly
    (C) Bi-Monthly (D) Annual
13. What is Bibliography
    (A) A list of books published
    (B) A list of books available in a library
    (C) A list of books available in two libraries
    (D) A list of Journals
14. who is regarded as father of bibliography?
    (A) Paul Otlet (B) Conrad Gesner
    (C) J. C. Brunet (D) A. C. Fosket.
15. Which type of publications are not excluded in Indian National Bibliography
    (A) Maps
    (B) Musical
    (C) Guides to textbook
    (D) First issue of Periodicals

16. The concept of Selective Dissemination of Information (SDI) was introduced by
    (A) Kaiser (B) Luhn of IBM
    (C) S. R. Ranganathan (D) Derek Austin.
17. Maps, Atlases can be categorised into
    (a) General or Topographic
    (b) Local
    (c) Special or Thematic
    (d) In series
    Codes:
    (A) (a), (b), and (c) (B) (a), (b), and (d)
    (C) (b), (c), and (d) (D) All of the above
18. which of the following is not an example of Current Awareness Service (CAS)?
    (A) SDI (B) An Indexing Bulletin
    (C) Current Contents (D) A Reading List
19. The author who defined Reference Service as the "Process of establishing contact between a reader and his documents in a personal way" is :
    (A) WA. Katz (B) L. Shores
    (C) M. Hutchins (D) S. R. Ranganathan
20. Orientation of library users is a kind of:
    (A) Reference Service
    (B) Referral Service
    (C) Current Awareness Service
    (D) Selective Dissemination of Information Service
21. **Assertion (A) :** Reference service is the hub of all library activities.
    Reason (R) : It is provided in the shortest possible time.
    (A) (A) is true, but (R) is false
    (B) (R) is true, but (A) is false
    (C) Both (A) and (R) are true, but (R) is not the right explanation of (A)

(D) Both (A) and (R) are true, and (R) is the right explanation

22. The term 'Bibliophile' refers to
    (A) a Bibliographer (B) a Book Lover
    (C) a Publisher (D) a Book Binder.
23. Non-bibliographic Database contain
    (A) Numeric Data (B) Textual Data
    (C) Visual Data (D) All of the above
24. MESH is the name of a
    (A) Medical Library
    (B) C.S.I.R Unit
    (C) Controlled Vocabulary
    (D) None of the above
25. which terms was coined by S.R. Ranganathan for mobile libraries
    (A) Moving library (B) Library on wheels
    (C) Library machine (D) All of the above
26. Which section of the library is known as hub of the staff ?
    (A) Maintenance section (B) Reference section
    (C) Circulation section (D) Technical section.
27. Geography deals with
    (a) the surface of the earth (continents and countries)
    (b) the climate,
    (c) plants, animals,
    (d) natural resources, people and industries

    Codes:
    (A) (a) only (B) (a) and (b)
    (C) (a), (b), and (c) (D) (a),(b),(c),and (d)
28. Which of the following names are associated with Post-Coordinate indexing

(A) Taube, Mooers, Batten
(B) Taube, Austin, Coats
(C) Taube, Austin, Garfield
(D) Mooers, Taube, Garfield

29. A map is a representation of certain boundaries of the earth on a flat surface showing
(a) countries (b) bodies of water
(c) cities
Codes:
(A) (a) and (b) (B) (a) and (c)
(C) (b) and (c) (D) (a), (b), and (c)

30. Publisher of Indian National Bibliography is
(A) Central Reference Library, Delhi
(B) Central Reference Library, Mumbai
(C) Central Reference Library, Kolkata
(D) Central Reference Library, Dehradun

31. Slic Indexing
(A) J.R.Sharp (B) M.Taube
(C) H.P.Luhn (D) E.J.Coates

32. There are a few basic factors which may be applied in winning the hearts of the readers. They are
(A) psychological factor, environmental factor, social factor
(B) self factor, psychological factor, service factor
(C) service factor, philosophical factor, self factor
(D) technological factor, service factor, self factor.

33. Periodicity of Indian National Bibliography is
(A) Weekly (B) Monthly
(C) Bi-Monthly (D) Quarterly.

34. Indexing system in which the coordination of terms is done at the search stage was first introduced by
(A) S.R. Ranganathan (B) Derek Austin
(C) Morfiner Taube (D) H.P. Luhn

35. Index Medicus is brought out as printed publication
    (A) Quarterly (B) Monthly
    (C) Weekly (D) Has ceased publication
36. **Assertion (A) :** ISBDs were devised by UNESCO.
    Reason (R) : They are the standards for all types of bibliographic activities.
    (A) (A) is false but (R) is true.
    (B) (A) is true but (R) is false.
    (C) Both (A) and (R) are true.
    (D) Both (A) and (R) are false.
37. **Assertion (A) :** Provision of services outside the library regular service centre or outlet is essential to reach more and more patrons.
    Reason (R) : Library extension services help libraries to cover larger population of patrons.
    (A) (A) is true but (R) is false.
    (B) (A) is false but (R) is true.
    (C) Both (A) and (R) are true.
    (D) Both (A) and (R) are false.
38. 'Union List' is the record of
    (A) Library members living in a Union Territory
    (B) Periodicals available in a group of libraries
    (C) Library unions located in a Union Territory
    (D) List of
39. Which of the follwing is/are example for general geographical sources of information
    (a) encyclopaedias
    (b) yearbooks and almanacs,
    (c) dictionaries,
    (d) statistical sources
    Codes:
    (A) (a) only (B) (a), (b), and (c)
    (C) (a),(b),(c),and (d) (D) (a), (b), and (d)

40. Auto abstracting involves use of computers to
    (A) structure the content of an abstract
    (B) prepare indicative abstract
    (C) pickup significant words
    (D) arrange words in order

41. An increase in the level of 'specificity' of indexing languages results in increase in
    (A) Recall
    (B) Precision
    (C) Noise
    (D) both recall and precision

42. **Assertion (A)** : A bibliographic utility is an organization that offers bibliographic services to subscribing libraries.

    Reason (R) : Library of Congress is a bibliographic utility.

    Codes :
    (A) (A) is true, but (R) is false.
    (B) (A) is false, but (R) is true.
    (C) Both (A) and (R) are true.
    (D) Both (A) and (R) are false.

43. Bibliographical coupling is related to
    (A) Bibliometric studies
    (B) Bibliography compilation
    (C) Modes of subject formation
    (D) Vocabulary control

44. A type of indexing where terms are coordinated prior to searching
    (A) Post coordinate indexing
    (B) Pre coordinate indexing
    (C) Uniterm indexing
    (D) None of the above

45. **Assertion (A) :** Deacidification is a measure to preserve documents in any medium.

    Reason (R) : Digital preservation needs a different preservation care.

    Codes :

    (A) (A) is false, but (R) is true.
    (B) (A) is true, but (R) is false.
    (C) Both (A) and (R) are true.
    (D) Both (A) and (R) are false.

46. **Assertion (A) :** SDI is a user oriented current information service.

    Reason (R) : It is an alerting service directed towards groups.

    Codes :

    (A) Both (A) and (R) are true.
    (B) (A) is true, but (R) is false.
    (C) (A) is false, but (R) is true.
    (D) Both (A) and (R) are false.

47. Retrospective search service is a type of

    (A) Referral service (B) Responsive service
    (C) CAS (D) SDI

48. What is the suitable reference sources to know about the information of a particular place?

    (A) Directory (B) Gazetteer
    (C) Encyclopedia (D) Year book

49. What is the suitable reference sources to find out the list of historical monuments of Delhi?

    (A) Atlas (B) Gazetteer
    (C) Guide book (D) Globe

50. An atlas is a collection of

    (a) maps (b) tables
    (c) charts

Codes :

(A) (a) and (b) (B) (a) and (c)

(C) (b) and (c) (D) (a), (b), and (c)

51. Which is not a functions of a bibliography?
    (A) It provides direction to researcher
    (B) It helps a librarian to be selective
    (C) It is not a systematic guide to the literature of the subject
    (D) Aids in locating information through the publishers

52. The person who provides reference service is called
    (A) Chief librarian (B) Grade One Librarian
    (C) Deputy Librarian (D) Reference Librarian

53. Identify parts of Social Science citation index
    (A) Corporate Index
    (B) Permuterm Subject Index
    (C) Source Index
    (D) Title Index

    Codes :
    (A) (B) and (C) are correct
    (B) (C) and (D) are correct
    (C) (D) and (A) are correct
    (D) (A) and (B) are correct

54. Reference and information service is most relevant to
    (A) Referral Service
    (B) SDI
    (C) CAS
    (D) Retrospective searching

55. Who had given the Minimal, Middling and Maximum theories of reference service?
    (A) C. M. Winchell (B) S. R. Ranganathan
    (C) James I Wyer (D) Samuel Rothstein

56. Select the advantages of Geographical Sources:
    (a) they give information for smaller units not found in general reference books
    (b) the information given often is more precise
    (c) they are generally limited to one area, and easier to use.

    Codes :

    (A) (a) only (B) (a) and (b)
    (C) (a) and (c) (D) (a), (b), and (c)

57. Who propounded Conservative, moderate and liberal theories of reference service?
    (A) William A Katz (B) S. R. Ranganathan
    (C) James I. Wyer (D) R. Emery

58. Zero based budget is concerned with
    (A) Present (B) Past
    (C) Future (D) Remote future

59. Indian National Bibliography index divided into
    (1) Classified part (2) Subject Index
    (3) Title Index (4) Author Index

    Codes :

    (A) 1,2,3 (B) 2,3,4
    (C) 1,2,4 (D) 1,3,4

60. The word 'bibliography' has originated from the .... terms - 'biblion' meaning a book and 'graphien' meaning to write
    (A) Greek (B) Latin
    (C) German (D) French

61. Which of the follwing is/are example for Specific geographical sources of information
    (a) maps, atlases and globes
    (b) gazetteers
    (c) travel guides

Codes:

(A) (a) only (B) (a) and (b)

(C) (a) and (c) (D) (a), (b), and (c)

62. Gazeteers can be categorised into

(a) International (b) National

(c) Topographic (d) Regional or Local

Codes :

(A) (a), (b), and (c) (B) (a), (b), and (d

(C) (b), (c), and (d) (D) All of the above

63. Travel Guides can be categorised into

(a) In Series (b) individual

(c) Regional (d) International

Codes:

(A) (a) and (b) (B) (a) and (c)

(C) (a) and (d) (D) (c) and (d)

64. The bibliography usually provides ...... to information

(A) multiple access points

(B) a single access point

(C) Double access points

(D) All the above

65. Bibliographic coupling was first advocated by

(A) B. K. Sen (B) M. M. Kessler

(C) S. C. Bradford (D) S. R. Ranganathan

66. Inductive logic proceeds from

(A) General to General (B) Particular to General

(C) General to Particular (D) Particular to Particular

67. What is the meaning of 'Translation Pools' ?

(A) Details about the names of translation experts

(B) Details about the addresses of the translators

(C) Agency of the names of translation experts

(D) None of these.

68. Reading centre's, story hours, exhibitions and reading to literature are forms of ...
    (A) Extension service
    (B) Service of a public library
    (C) Both
    (D) None
69. the bibliography is the chief class or form of reference and information access tools
    (A) Yes (B) No
    (C) Sometime (D) Never
70. "Reference service is the contact between the right reader and the right book in the right personal way" was stated by...
    (A) D J Fockett
    (B) S R Ranganathan
    (C) James I Wyer
    (D) A.L.A Glossary of library terms

INDEXING SYSTEMS AND THEIR CONTRIBUTOR

S.No.	*Indexing Systems*	*Inventor*
1	Chain Index	S. R. Ranganathan
2	Precis	Derek Austin
3	Popsi	G.bhattacharya
4	Uniterm Indexing	M. Taube
5	Keyword Indexing	H.P.Luhn
6	Citation Indexing	Eugine Garfield
7	Subject Indexing	M.E.Sears
8	Slic Indexing	R.Sharp
9	Automatic Indexing	Herbert Ohlman
10	Thesauras	P.M.Roget

ANSWERS

1 (B)	2 (C)	3 (D)	4 (A)	5 (D)	6 (D)
7 (C)	8 (C)	9 (D)	10 (D)	11 (A)	12 (A)
13 (A)	14 (B)	15 (D)	16 (B)	17 (A)	18 (D)
19 (A)	20 (A)	21 (C)	22 (B)	23 (D)	24 (C)
25 (B)	26 (A)	27 (D)	28 (D)	29 (D)	30 (C)
31 (A)	32 (D)	33 (B)	34 (B)	35 (B)	36 (A)
37 (C)	38 (B)	39 (C)	40 (A)	41 (B)	42 (C)
43 (A)	44 (B)	45 (A)	46 (B)	47 (B)	48 (B)
49 (C)	50 (D)	51 (C)	52 (D)	53 (A)	54 (D)
55 (D)	56 (D)	57 (C)	58 (C)	59 (C)	60 (A)
61 (D)	62 (B)	63 (A)	64 (B)	65 (B)	66 (B)
67 (C)	68 (C)	69 (A)	70 (B)		

Information Services

1. Universal Bibliographical Control's is a programme of:
   (A) ALA (B) FID
   (C) IFLA (D) UNISIST
2. The User Profile is a
   (A) List of descriptors
   (B) List of Useful citations
   (C) List of Users
   (D) Statements of user information
3. UAP was launched by
   (A) ILA (B) IFLA
   (C) LA (D) ICSU
4. Delhi public library was established as a pilot project with the assistance from
   (A) U.N.O (B) F.I.D
   (C) U.N.I.D.O (D) U.N.E.S.C.O
5. Shelf list facilitates.................
   (A) Classification (B) Weeding out
   (C) Stock verification (D) Documentation
6. The 'Five Laws of Library Science' propounded by Dr. S. R. Ranganathan, is which type of research?
   (A) Applied research (B) Pure research
   (C) Basic research (D) Survey research.
7. Information Science is a discipline that investigates
   (A) the properties and behaviour of information
   (B) the forces governing the flow of information
   (C) the means for processing of information for optimal uses
   (D) all of these.

8. Which record is the hub of the stack in a library?
   (A) Accession register (B) Shelf list register
   (C) Book catalogue (D) Staff manual.
9. Who contributed on the systematic use of user's education?
   (A) S.S.Green (B) Melvil Dewey
   (C) E. J. Coates (D) Patricia B. Knapp.
10. The resource sharing strategy of a library may not include
    (A) joint acquisition 2.
    (B) shared use
    (C) exchange of materials
    (D) restricted access
11. Invisible colleges are
    (A) networks of people interested in the same subject
    (B) help in communication
    (C) neither (1) nor (2)
    (D) both (1) and (2)
12. Herald of Library Science is published from
    (A) Delhi (B) Lucknow
    (C) Culcutta (D) Banaras
13. Information is a part of
    (A) Information Science
    (B) Scientific achievement
    (C) Knowledge
    (D) Communication
14. Resource sharing is a part of ...
    (A) Library cooperation (B) Library administration
    (C) Library management (D) Library cataloguing
15. Universal Copyright Convention of 1952 was held at
    (A) Geneva (B) Delhi
    (C) New York (D) Burlin

16. CAS, SDI, Indexing & Abstracting and Literature Searching Service
    (A) Bibliographical service
    (B) Reference Service
    (C) Indexing Service
    (D) None of the above
17. Who used the term 'Technical Service' at first
    (A) S R Ranganathan (B) Jack Mills
    (C) William Ewart (D) Maurie F Taube.
18. The term 'Precision'to measure the performance of Information Retrieval Systems, was suggested by:
    (A) S.R. Ranganathan (B) F.W. Lancastere
    (C) Cyril Cleverdon (D) H.P. Luhn
19. User education may be provided in four interrelated areas which are
    (A) user's awareness, user studies, library orientation, bibliographic instruction
    (B) user's awareness, library orientation, inter-profiling, bibliographic instruction
    (C) aptitude test of the users, use of cataloguing, inter-profiling, user's awareness
    (D) bibliographic instruction, library orientation, computer literacy, user's awareness.
20. the first systematic training of Librarians in India was started by
    (A) Asa Don Dickinson (B) KM Asadullah
    (C) W.A.Bordon (D) S.R.Rangnathan
21. Preparation, service and assimilation are the main stages involved in
    (A) Initiation (B) User Education
    (C) Reference Service (D) Bibliography
22. CAS is defined as

(A) A process of dissemination of information
(B) A process of information
(C) A process of dissemination of current information
(D) A simple information service

23. The biggest library in the world is
(A) Lenin state library
(B) Bibliotheca Nationale
(C) Library of congress
(D) British Meuseum

24. Which service demands the creation of a 'user' profile?
(A) CAS (B) Information retrieval
(C) SDI (D) Reference service

25. INSDOC established in__________with technical assistance from UNESCO
(A) 1950 (B) 1951
(C) 1952 (D) 1953

26. Providing information on the basis of an expressed demand is called
(A) responsive services (B) anticipatory services
(C) Demand services (D) All the above

27. ISBN consists of
(A) ten digits (B) thirteen digits
(C) 8-bytes (D) there are no digits.

28. INSDOC was established in the year
(A) 1948 (B) 1952
(C) 1960 (D) 1967

29. ASK (Approach, Skill, Knowledge) principle is related to
(A) classification (B) management
(C) ICT (D) standards.

30. Which section of the library is known as hub of the staff?

(A) Maintenance section (B) Reference section
(C) Circulation section (D) Technical section.

31. IPR stands for
(A) Indian Press Registration
(B) Intellectual Property Right
(C) International Property Right
(D) Indian Property Regulations.

32. India Office is located at
(A) Culcutta (B) London
(C) Bonbay (D) Paris

33. NSDOC is functioning under the Council of Scientific and Industrial Research (CSIR), which is an autonomous body under the
(A) Ministry of Culture
(B) Ministry of Science and Technology
(C) Ministry of Human Resources Development
(D) Ministry of Environment and Forests

34. Resources sharing among libraries was prompted by the factors
(A) Price escalation
(B) Information explosion
(C) Both (A) and (B)
(D) None of the above

35. Real Time Access refers to
(A) Access in advance
(B) Access after some time
(C) Access when searched for
(D) None of the above

36. The name of Imperial Library (Indian) was changed to National Library in the year
(A) 1947 (B) 1948
(C) 1950 (D) 1952

37. Forms of Extension service
    (A) Library Websites
    (B) Library Orientation
    (C) Book fair and Exhibition
    (D) All
38. Cover to cover translation is treated as
    (A) Selective dissemination service
    (B) Current awareness services
    (C) On demand services
    (D) Anticipatory services
39. Which terms was coined by S.R. Ranganathan for mobile libraries
    (A) Moving library (B) Library on wheels
    (C) Library machine (D) All of the above
40. Abstracting service provides…
    (A) Abstract of articles
    (B) Whole bibliographic description of articles
    (C) Whole bibliographic description along with abstracts of article
    (D) Whole bibliographic sources
41. Reference questions of fact- finding nature is called
    (A) Directional guidance
    (B) Ready reference service
    (C) Long range reference service
    (D) General help
42. The basic information role of a library is to
    (A) Give away books to the library users
    (B) Collect and disseminate information
    (C) Collect all information available in print media
    (D) Collect information in non-print media
43. The professional requirement for the reference staff is

(A) knowledge of reference source
(B) their contents
(C) organisation and presentation
(D) All the above

44. Feedback mechanism is a part of which service?
(A) Reprography service
(B) CAS
(C) Translation service
(D) SDI

45. Mobile library is a kind of which service?
(A) Reference service
(B) Extension service
(C) Ready reference service
(D) Long range reference service

46. Reading centre, story hours, exhibition and reading to literature are form of
(A) Extension service (B) Service of Public library
(C) Both (D) None

47. The three broad categories of books are
(A) Reference Books. Text Books, Handbooks
(B) Books on Information, Recreation, Inspiration
(C) Books on Knowledge, Information, Data
(D) Books for Children, Middle, Aged, Old Aged

48. The marketing concepts in Library Service include
(A) analysis, planning, implementation and control
(B) advertising, planning, analysis and control
(C) distribution, control, analysis, implementation
(D) indexing, planning, control and implementation

49. Possible Reference Source for Technical terms in different subjects
(A) Language dictionaries (B) Thesauri
(C) Special glossaries. (D) Bibliographies

50. Which is not a principle way in which requests for documents or information may reach the reference division of a library.
   (A) Personal visit by user
   (B) Telephone call
   (C) Written communication
   (D) Current awareness service

51. Which one is Library and Information Science Journal name?
   (A) Reference Reviews incorporating ASLIB Book Guide
   (B) Reference Reviews incorporating ASLIB Book journals
   (C) Reference Reviews incorporating ASLIB Book Review
   (D) Reference Reviews incorporating ASLIB E-Book

52. "Shodhganga" is a national level repository of
   (A) E-Books (B) E-Journals
   (C) E-Theses (D) Journal Articles

53. The national library of India was declared to open on 1st February 1953 by
   (A) Dr. Rajendra Prasad
   (B) Dr. S. Radha Krishnan
   (C) Jawaharlal Nehru
   (D) Maulana AbdulKalam Azad

54. Informal self education is possible in what kind of library?
   (A) National Library (B) Public Library
   (C) Specific Library (D) College Library

55. The Chairman of the National Knowledge Commission, Govt. of India, is
   (A) D. P. Chattopadhyay (B) B. P. Barua
   (C) R. K. Dasgupta (D) Dr. Sam Pitroda

56. A user may want to look at all the information that has been published on a given topic

    1. Everyday Approach 2. Exhaustive Approach
    3. Current Approach 4. Comprehensive

    (A) 1 and 3 (B) 2 and 4
    (C) 2 Only (D) 4 only

57. Which network in India provided the first e-mail service in the country?

    (A) NICNET (B) ERNET
    (C) INFLIBNET (D) DELNET

58. An appropriate source to find out descriptive information is................ .

    (A) Bibliography (B) Directory
    (C) Encyclopedia (D) Dictionary

59. Glossary is a

    (A) List of technical words with definitions
    (B) List of words in a language
    (C) List of thematically arranged words
    (D) Alphabetical index to passages of work

60. Who among the following honoured with 'Nobel Prize' for his substantial contribution in Documentation ?

    (A) S. C. Bradford (B) Loosjes
    (C) Eric De Grolier (D) Henri La Fontaine

61. The Farmington plan is associated with

    (A) Library Legislation
    (B) Library Cataloguing
    (C) Library Cooperation
    (D) Library Indexing Service

62. National Science Library is an integral unit of

    (A) INSDOC (B) DESIDOC
    (C) NASSDOC (D) SENDOC

63. International Information System on Research in Documentation (ISORID) was established by

(A) IFLA (B) UNESCO
(C) SLA (D) ALA

64. What is the relationship between ISBD and cataloguing codes?
(A) They are not related at all
(B) Cataloguing codes will include bibliographic description
(C) ISBD includes cataloguing rules
(D) ISBD can replace cataloguing rules

65. In which year did A. W. Borden start a refresher course for librarians in India ?
(A) 1905 (B) 1910
(C) 1912 (D) 1913.

66. Resource sharing among the libraries was originally known as
(A) Inter Library Loan (B) Library Cooperation
(C) Library Networking (D) Material Sharing

67. OCLC currently stands for :
(A) Online Computer Library Centre
(B) Ohio College Library Centre
(C) Online Centre of Library of Congress
(D) Online Cataloging of Library of Congress

68. Who said 'some books are to be tasted, others to be swallowed and some few to be chewed and digested'?
(A) John Milton (B) William Jones
(C) Francis Bacon (D) Benjamin Franklin

69. In which year was the International Book Year celebrated by UNESCO?
(A) 1931 (B) 1947
(C) 1952 (D) 1972.

70. Reading centre's, story hours, exhibitions and reading to literature are forms of ...

(A) Extension service
(B) Service of a public library
(C) Both
(D) None

71. The term 'Information Retrieval' is coined by
(A) Calvin Mooers (B) S R Ranganathan
(C) H P Luhan (D) J D Brown

72. Which one of the following is the first biographical dictionary
(A) Who was who (B) Who's who
(C) Both (D) None of them

73. Who coined the term 'informatics' in 1962
(A) Philippe Dreyfus (B) S R Ranganathan
(C) J E L Farradane (D) Frits Donker Duyvis

74. Current Awareness Service has come in
(A) 1950's (B) 1960's
(C) 1970's (D) 1940's

75. The National Library of Medicine is one of the three national libraries in the
(A) UK (B) India
(C) USA (D) Canada

76. How many kinds of reference service Dr. Ranganathan recognize
(A) 2 (B) 3
(C) 4 (D) 12

77. In which year H P Luhan introduced the SDI
(A) 1961 (B) 1956
(C) 1984 (D) 1958

78. MEDLARS has been in use since
(A) 1962 (B) 1964
(C) 1972 (D) 1974

79. NISSAT came to be established as a project under Plan of the Fifth Five-Year Plan

(A) Second Five-Year Plan
(B) Third Five-Year Plan
(C) Fourth Five-Year Plan
(D) Fifth Five-Year Plan

80. Technonet Asia for Industrial Information, is located in
(A) China (B) India
(C) Singapore (D) Thailand

81. CAS and SDI are example of
(A) Extension Services
(B) Document Delivery Service
(C) Alerting Service
(D) Literature Search Service

82. UGC has established the National Centre for Science Information (NCSI) at the
(A) National Science Library, Delhi
(B) Indian Institute of Technology, Chennai
(C) MS University, Baroda
(D) Indian Institute of Science, Bangalore

83. The user tries to keep himself abreast of what is being published from time to time in his area of specialisation
(A) Everyday Approach
(B) Exhaustive Approach
(C) Current Approach
(D) Comprehensive Approach

84. Deference questions of fact- finding nature is called
(A) Directional guidance
(B) Ready reference service
(C) Long range reference service
(D) General help

85. While entering the library, the personal belongings of a reader is kept in

(A) Cloak Room (B) Property Counter

(C) Gate Counter (D) Store Room

Read the passage below and answer the questions based on understanding of the passage. (Answer 86-90 questions)

Communication media have evolved along with technological transformations and progress. Man's inborn need to communicate led to the first medium for the global transmission of nformation – the printing press, followed by the rotary printing press. But the need for information has always been in continuous growth, so that inventions such as telegraph had to be adopted for information transmission by waves. Indeed, the radio was one of the society's great technological and democratizing advances. But there is no doubt that television has succeeded in making McLuhan's idea of the existence of a television tribe a reality. Large companies, which control access to information by methods that are close to being a monopoly, wage fierce battles in order to control mass media, especially television.

The "fourth power" collects, disseminates and preserves a great quantity of information. This information is thematically diverse and exists in a wide variety of formats and media. In order to control such an important business asset, almost all television broadcasters have set a documentation service that is responsible for satisfying journalists' information needs and for the maintenance of the firm's intellectual and cultural heritage. Documentation centres are just the visible aspects of a great documentation web involving different classes of documents, varied media and the diverse requirements of end users. The computerization of documentation structures is a reality that is sustained by a constant exchange of information between documenta lists and communication scientists, aimed at enabling the preservation of information and access to this information by means of a standard set of parameters.

The thematic descriptors must describe, viewed and

referred content in the audiovisual documents with precision. Thematic identification has a special importance since it is the usual method for accessing information. For these fields, different television companies use different proprietary ad hoe tools, with thesauri being the formula employed to control vocabulary. There have also been experiments aimed at developing effective tools based on faceted classifications. The fact that audio-visual information has to be analysed from two different perspectives in order to understand the challenges offered by this kind of document should be considered. The visual and the sonorous sometimes are complementary, and consequently must be studied and analysed by the information manager. Sound and visual tracks do often collaborate to create a joint informative message, but it is also very common the case where both contribute to create quite different meanings.

86. The first medium for global transmission of information was_______.
   (A) Radio (B) Printing Press
   (C) Television (D) Telegraph

87. The intellectual and cultural heritage of television broadcasting firms is maintained by
   (A) Communication media
   (B) Journalists
   (C) Television
   (D) Setting up a documentation service

88. A standard set of parameters is needed for _______.
   (A) Establishing documentation centres
   (B) Meeting diverse requirements of users
   (C) Preservation and access to information
   (D) Exchange of documents

89. For organizing information, television companies use tools such as

(A) Thesaurus
(B) Faceted classification
(C) Non-faceted classification
(D) Thematic descriptors

90. Audio-visual information has to be analyzed for
(A) Information management
(B) Understanding the challenges offered by such documents
(C) Collaborating sound and visual tracks
(D) Locating information from different places

91. The UNESCO Definition for Public Library is Popularly known as :
(A) The Place of continuous learning
(B) UNESCO Public Library
(C) UNESCO Public Library Manifesto
(D) Modern Public Library Manifesto

ANSWERS

1 (B)	2 (D)	3 (B)	4 (D)	5 (C)	6 (C)
7 (D)	8 (A)	9 (D)	10 (A)	11 (D)	12 (B)
13 (A)	14 (A)	15 (A)	16 (A)	17 (D)	18 (B)
19 (A)	20 (C)	21 (C)	22 (C)	23 (C)	24 (C)
25 (C)	26 (A)	27 (B)	28 (B)	29 (B)	30 (A)
31 (B)	32 (B)	33 (B)	34 (C)	35 (C)	36 (B)
37 (D)	38 (B)	39 (B)	40 (C)	41 (B)	42 (B)
43 (D)	44 (D)	45 (B)	46 (C)	47 (B)	48 (B)
49 (C)	50 (D)	51 (A)	52 (C)	53 (D)	54 (B)
55 (D)	56 (B)	57 (D)	58 (C)	59 (A)	60 (D)
61 (C)	62 (A)	63 (B)	64 (D)	65 (B)	66 (A)
67 (B)	68 (C)	69 (D)	70 (C)	71 (A)	72 (B)
73 (A)	74 (A)	75 (C)	76 (C)	77 (D)	78 (B)
79 (D)	80 (C)	81 (C)	82 (D)	83 (C)	84 (B)
85 (B)	86 (B)	87 (D)	88 (C)	89 (A)	90 (A)
91 (C)					

5
Classification and Cataloguing

CLASSIFICATION SCHEMES AND YEAR OF PUBLICATION

S.No	*Classification Schemes*	*Year*
1	Dewey Decimal Classification	1876
2	Expansive Classification	1891
3	Library of congress Classification	1904
4	Universal Decimal Classification	1905
5	Subject Classification	1906
6	Colon classification	1933
7	Bibliographic Classification	1935
8	Riders International Classification	1961
9	Broad System of Ordering	1978

1. The Standard size of a catalogue card is
   (A) 5 inch x 4 inch (B) 5 inch x 3inch
   (C) 5 inch x 5 inch (D) 3 inch x 5 inch
2. Classification of all types of libraries has been made by-
   (A) IFLA (B) UNISIST
   (C) UNESCO (D) INSDOC

3. According to CCC, the heading for work with three authors is
   (A) The first author (B) The title
   (C) The principal author (D) All the three authors
4. Which of the following areas is not a part of the description prescribed by AACR-II?
   (A) Title and statement of responsibility area
   (B) Edition
   (C) Publication and distribution
   (D) Address and location
5. Paul Otlet used the term [illegible] time in a lecture at the Intern[illegible] Brussels in
   (A) 1907 (B) 1920
   (C) 1931 (D) 1948
6. which library first introduced the printed catalog
   (A) British Museum (B) Library of Congress
   (C) Lelin State (D) Imperial Library
7. Sear's List of Subject Headings (SLSH) is mainly useful for
   (A) Small and medium libraries
   (B) Special libraries
   (C) Academic libraries
   (D) College libraries
8. ______________ is one of the records of circulation Section
   (A) Accession Register (B) Day Book
   (C) Catalogue Card (D) AACR-2
9. Dewey decimal classification is a
   (A) Alphabetical scheme
   (B) Numerical scheme
   (C) Alphanumerical scheme
   (D) None of the above

10. The CCF was developed by
    (A) LC (B) UNESCO
    (C) IFLA (D) FID

11. Vatican Code (VC)
    (A) 1927 (B) 1928
    (C) 1929 (D) 1930

12. which table deals with 'Standard Subdivisions' in DDC?
    (B) Table 3
    (D) Table 7

...stands for
    (A) ...ject of Organisation
    (B) Broad Subject Ordering
    (C) Bibliography of Subject Ordering
    (D) Bibliographic Subject Organisation.

14. Pre-natal Cataloguing means:
    (A) Simplified Cataloguing
    (B) Pre-Publication Cataloguing
    (C) Selective Cataloguing
    (D) Shared Cataloguing

15. which of the following would be the correct chronological sequence?
    (A) Bibliometrics, Informetrics, Librametry, Webometrics
    (B) Librametry, Bibliometrics, Informetrics, Webometrics
    (C) Librametry, Informetrics, Bibliometrics, Webometrics
    (D) Bibliometrics, Informetrics, Webometrics, Librametry

16. Arrange the physical forms of catalogue in the chronological sequence :

(A) Register, Sheaf Catalogue, Card Catalogue, OPAC
(B) Sheaf Catalogue, Register, Card Catalogue, OPAC
(C) Card Catalogue, Sheaf Catalogue, Register, OPAC
(D) Sheaf Catalogue, Card Catalogue, Register, OPAC

17. Which is the oldest classification scheme in the following

(A) UDC (B) DDC
(C) EC (D) CCC

18. Match the following:

List-I (Work)	**List-II (Author)**
(a) Subject Classification	(i) J. Atchinson
(b) Thesauro facet	(ii) C.A. Cutter
(c) Classified Catalogue Code	(iii) J.D. Brown
(d) Rules for Dictionary Catalogue	(iv) S.R. Ranganathan

Code :	**(a)**	**(b)**	**(c)**	**(d)**
(A)	(iii)	(i)	(iv)	(ii)
(B)	(ii)	(iii)	(i)	(iv)
(C)	(iv)	(ii)	(iii)	(i)
(D)	(i)	(ii)	(iii)	(iv)

19. Ontology is................. .

(A) An Indexing Method
(B) Classification of Internet based documents
(C) Cataloguing of Internet based documents
(D) Documentation service

20. In CC, the principle that helps in the identification of personality category is

(A) Cow-calf principle (B) Whole-organ principle
(C) Neti-neti principle (D) Later-in-time principle

21. In DDC Phoenix schedules represent
    (A) classes which are slightly modified
    (B) classes which are completely changed
    (C) classes to be modified in the future
    (D) classes not to be modified

22. What is the relationship between ISBD and Cataloguing Codes?
    (A) They are not related at all
    (B) Cataloguing codes will include bibliographic description
    (C) ISBD includes cataloguing rules
    (D) ISBD can replace cataloguing codes

23. which of the following combinations is wrong
    (A) PRECIS-Dreck Austin-BNB
    (B) KWIC-H.P. Luhn-Chemical titles
    (C) Citation Indexing-Eugene Garfield-SCI
    (D) Relational indexing-E.J. Coates-Biological Abstracts

24. A document description is not found in a
    (A) Catalogue entry (B) Citation
    (C) Bibliographic entry (D) **Class number**

25. According to AACR-II, the heading of the main entry for conference proceeding edited by an individual is prepared under
    (A) name of editor (B) place of conference
    (C) title of the volume (D) name of the conference

26. In UDC the inter-relationship between the two subjects is denoted by
    (A) Ampersand followed by Roman Smalls
    (B) Colon
    (C) Double Colon
    (D) Hyphen

27. The table standard subdivision helps a classification scheme
    (A) to ensure consistency
    (B) to add mnemonic value
    (C) both the above
    (D) None of the above
28. Rules for dictionary catalogue were devised by:
    (A) A. Pannizzi (B) C. C. Jewet
    (C) S. Lubetzky (D) C. A. Cutter
29. CCF stands for.
    (A) Current Classification Format
    (B) Current Communication Format
    (C) Common Communication Format
    (D) Common Classification Format
30 Prussion Instruction
    (A) 1900 (B) 1899
    (C) 1898 (D) 1897
31. CRG stands for :
    (A) Committee for Rural Grant
    (B) Classification Research Group
    (C) Committee for Ranganathan Guild
    (D) Classic Research Grant
32. Anglo-American Code (AAC)
    (A) 1908 (B) 1907
    (C) 1906 (D) 1905
33. Three great achievements in U.S.A. were noticed i.e. enunciation of DDC classification scheme, formation of American Library Association and the publication of 1 st Journal of the librarianship in the year
    (A) 1857 (B) 1859
    (C) 1876 (D) 1901.
34. WorldCat is maintained by

(A) Library of Congress
(B) Online Computer Library Center
(C) American Library Association
(D) None of the above

35. 260 tag in MARC format marks
(A) The edition
(B) The publication information
(C) The physical description
(D) A topical subject heading

36. **Assertion (A) :** Web OPAC is a computerised library catalogue available to the patrons online.
Reason (R) : It can be searched by the users within the four walls of the library only.
(A) (A) is true but (R) is false.
(B) (A) is false but (R) is true.
(C) Both (A) and (R) are true.
(D) Both (A) and (R) are false.

37. The Principle of Local Variation is mainly applicable in
(A) Cataloguing (B) Reference service
(C) Circulation (D) Acquisition

38. who is the author of "Subject Catalogue" ?
(A) E. J. Coates (B) J. Kaiser
(C) C. A. Cutter (D) J. W. Metcalfe

39. **Assertion (A) :** In Colon Classification, 2 represents mother country and 44 represents India. A given library in India can use 2 or 44 for India.
Reason (R) : The above is in conformity with Canon of Homonym.
Codes :
(A) Both (A) and (R) are true and (R) is the correct explanation of (A).

(B) Both (A) and (R) are true but (R) is not the correct explanation of (A).

(C) (A) is true, but (R) is false.

(D) (A) is false, but (R) is true.

40. **Assertion (A) :** In library classification, an empty digit helps in interpolation between two consecutive ordinal numbers.

Reason (R) : An empty digit is a digit with ordinal value but no semantic value.

Codes :

(A) Both (A) and (R) are true and (R) is the correct explanation of (A).

(B) Both (A) and (R) are true, but (R) is not a correct explanation of (A).

(C) (A) is true, but (R) is false.

(D) (A) is false, but (R) is true.

41. Arrange the following subjects in ascending order according to their DDC numbers:

(i) Horticulture (ii) Public Administration

(iii) Metaphysics (iv) Botany Codes :

Codes :

(A) (i), (iv), (iii), (ii) (B) (iii), (ii), (iv), (i)

(C) (ii), (iii), (i), (iv) (D) (iv), (ii), (i), (iii)

42. what will be the correct sequence of books on the shelves bearing the following class numbers?

(i) 2:51 (ii) 232

(iii) 2;46 (iv) 2'N65

Codes :

(A) (i), (ii), (iii), (iv) (B) (ii), (i), (iii), (iv)

(C) (iv), (i), (iii), (ii) (D) (iii), (iv), (ii), (i)

43. Arrange the following classification schemes according to their year of first publication:

(i) DDC (ii) CC

(iii) UDC (iv) LC

Codes :

(A) (i), (iv), (iii), (ii) (B) (i), (iv), (ii), (iii)

(C) (i), (ii), (iii), (iv) (D) (ii), (i), (iv), (iii)

44. **Assertion (A) :** Dewey Decimal is an enumerative scheme of classification.

    Reason (R) : The scheme has developed several devices and is no more an enumerative scheme of classification.

    Codes :

    (A) (A) is true, but (R) is false.

    (B) (A) is not true, but (R) is true.

    (C) Both (A) and (R) are true.

    (D) Both (A) and (R) are false.

45. Which is not a near synonym term to information?

    (A) Ideas (B) Data

    (C) Catalogue (D) Facts

46. Dewey Decimal classification is now looked after by

    (A) Lake Placid Club

    (B) OCLC

    (C) Library of Congress

    (D) Classification Research Group

47. Resource sharing is a part of

    (A) Library cooperation

    (B) Library Administration

    (C) Library Management

    (D) Library Cataloging

48. Arrange the following schemes of classification according to their year of publication:

    (i) CC (ii) DDC

    (iii) LC (iv) UDC

    Codes :

    (A) (ii), (i), (iii), (iv) (B) (ii), (iii), (iv), (i)

    (C) (i), (ii), (iv), (iii) (D) (iv), (iii), (ii), (i)

49. who Invented the Dictionary Catalogue?
    (A) Dr. S. R. Ranganathan
    (B) C. A. Cutter
    (C) D. B. Krishna Rao
    (D) K. N. Raj

50. what is the another name of Added entries?
    (A) Main entry
    (B) Cross reference entry
    (C) Secondary entries
    (D) Subject entry

51. when was SLSH published?
    (A) 1903 (B) 1897
    (C) 1923 (D) 1933

52. when was MARC project completed?
    (A) 1987 (B) 1967
    (C) 1947 (D) 1968

53. who enunciated the subject Classification
    (A) J. D. Brown
    (B) W. C. Sayers
    (C) Benjamin A.Custer
    (D) Frist Donker Duyvis

54. How many Auxiliary tables are there in DDC 23rd Edition
    (A) 16 (B) 6
    (C) 7 (D) 8

55. Colon classification was first published in
    (A) 1905 (B) 1931
    (C) 1933 (D) 1944

56. Phoenix schedules are part of which classification
    (A) CC (B) DDC
    (C) UDC (D) LCC

57. British Museum Code

(A) 1839 (B) 1840
(C) 1842 (D) 1841

58. In which year DDC 23rd edition was published
(A) 2000 (B) 2011
(C) 2003 (D) 2010

59. The word classification comes from the Latin word
(A) Classis (B) Classes
(C) Clauses (D) Fiction

60. The first edition of DDC published in
(A) 1875 (B) 1876
(C) 1874 (D) 1896

61. The first edition of UDC published in
(A) 1904 (B) 1901
(C) 1905 (D) 1894

62. who is the publishers of Sear's list of subject headings
(A) Dr. S. R. Ranganathan
(B) Brown
(C) H. W. Wilson
(D) C. A. Cutter

63. The First edition of DDC Consisted of
(A) 144 pages (B) Four volume
(C) 44 pages (D) 124 pages

64. What are the four entity of FRBR Model?
(A) Personality, Matter, Energy, Space
(B) Work, Expression, Manifestation, Item
(C) Book, Form, Availability, Type
(D) Discipline, Entity, Action, Personality

65. who is the Editor in Chief of 23rd Edition of DDC
(A) Benjamin A. Custer (B) John P. Comaromi
(C) Winton E. Matthews (D) John S. Mitchell

66. When was the different typological study towards mode of formation of subjects done?

(A) 1950 (B) 1960
(C) 1970 (D) 1975

67. In which edition "Auxiliary table for area" was first introduced?
(A) DDC 14 (C) DDC 16
(B) DDC 15 (D) DDC 17

68. What does LED stands for in CC?
(A) Latest Energy Developments
(B) Latest Effective Decade
(C) Large Energy Distribution
(D) Lowest Effective Decade

69. The term prenatal cataloguing first used by
(A) Michael Gorman
(B) Dr. S.R.Ranganathan
(C) E.B.Ross
(D) Melvin Dewey

70. The Dewey Decimal Classification divides human knowledge into
(A) 10 basic categories.
(B) 100 basic categories.
(C) 1000 basic categories.
(D) 10000 basic categories.

71. who devised Dewey Decimal Classification (DDC) System?
(A) Melville Dewey
(B) Dr. S. R. Ranganathan
(C) Tim Berners-Lee
(D) Vint Cerf

72. Call Number of a Book Means
(A) Book Number
(B) Class Number
(C) Both (A) and (B) are true
(D) None of the above

73. Accession Number means
    (A) Call Number of a book
    (B) Unique Number for a book inside a particular library.
    (C) Book Number
    (D) Class number

74. who is the Editor in Chief of 20th Edition of DDC
    (A) Benjamin A. Custer (B) John P. Comaromi
    (C) Winton E. Matthews (D) John S. Mitchell

75. who is the Editor in Chief of 21st Edition of DDC
    (A) Benjamin A. Custer (B) John P. Comaromi
    (C) Winton E. Matthews (D) John S. Mitchell

76. Who is the Editor in Chief of 22nd Edition of DDC
    (A) Benjamin A. Custer (B) John P. Comaromi
    (C) Winton E. Matthews (D) John S. Mitchell

77. Main use of Shelf list is
    (A) Cataloging (B) Circulation
    (C) Stock Verification (D) Book Selection

78. Who introduced Three card system
    (A) Krishan Kumar (B) C. K. Sharma
    (C) Cutter (D) S. R. Ranganathan

79. ________ are the storage areas for the various types of documents kept in a library.
    (A) Tasks (B) Racks
    (C) Stacks (D) Desks

80. Library catalogue cards are filed in specially designed. drawers called ________
    (A) Charging tray (B) Catalogue cabinet
    (C) Display rack (D) Filling equipment

81. The three card system introduced by Ranganathan are
    (i) Register Card (ii) Check Card
    (iii) ……..

(A) KARDEX (B) LINDEX
(C) Ledger Card (D) Classified Index Card

82. Technical section performs mainly two functions namely classification and
(A) accessioning (B) bills payment
(C) cataloguing (D) shelving

83. Getting books back from the users and releasing the borrower's ticket is known as
(A) charging (B) holding
(C) reserving (D) **discharging**

84. Match the following :

List – I	List – II
(a) C.A. Cutter	(i) Bibliographic Classification
(b) J.D. Brown	(ii) Expansive Classification
(c) S.R.Ranganathan	(iii) Subject Classification
(d) H.E. Bliss	(iv) Colon Classification

Code :	(a)	(b)	(c)	(d)
(A)	(ii)	(iii)	(iv)	(i)
(B)	(i)	(ii)	(iii)	(iv)
(C)	(iv)	(i)	(ii)	(iii)
(D)	(iii)	(ii)	(iv)	(i)

85. match the following:

List – I	List – II
(a) C.A. Cutter	(i) Bibliographic classification
(b) H.E. Bliss	(ii) Expansive classification
(c) J.D. Brown	(iii) Universal classification
(d) Paul Otlet & Henry LaFontaine	(iv) Subject classification

Code :	(a)	(b)	(c)	(d)
(A)	(ii)	(i)	(iv)	(iii)
(B)	(ii)	(iii)	(iv)	(i)
(C)	(i)	(iii)	(iv)	(ii)
(D)	(iii)	(iv)	(ii)	(i)

86. Match the following :

	List – I	List – II
(a)	International Conference on Cataloguing Principles	(i) 1969
(b)	International Meeting of Cataloguing Experts	(ii) 1961
(c)	International Symposium of Bibliographic Exchange format	(iii) 1990
(d)	First CCF Users meeting	(iv) 1978

Code :	(a)	(b)	(c)	(d)
(A)	**(ii)**	**(i)**	**(iv)**	**(iii)**
(B)	(iii)	(ii)	(iv)	(i)
(C)	(iv)	(iii)	(i)	(ii)
(D)	(iii)	(i)	(iv)	(ii)

87. Match the following :

	List – I	List – II
(a)	Elements of Library Classification	(i) D.J. Desolla Price
(b)	Little Science Big Science	(ii) S.R. Ranganathan
(c)	Documentation	(iii) D.J. Fosket
(d)	Subject Approach to Information	(iv) S.C. Bradford

Code :	(a)	(b)	(c)	(d)
(A)	(ii)	(i)	(iv)	(iii)
(B)	(iii)	(ii)	(i)	(iv)
(C)	(iv)	(ii)	(iii)	(i)
(D)	(i)	(ii)	(iii)	(iv)

88. Match the following :

	List – I	List – II
(a)	AACR-1	(i) 1978
(b)	AACR-2	(ii) 1967
(c)	ALA code	(iii) 1934
(d)	CCC	(iv) 1949

Code :	**(a)**	**(b)**	**(c)**	**(d)**
(A)	(iv)	(ii)	(iii)	(i)
(B)	(ii)	(i)	(iii)	(iv)
(C)	(i)	(iii)	(iv)	(ii)
(D)	(ii)	(i)	(iv)	(iii)

89. Rules for Dictionary Catalogue (RDC)
    (A) 1879 (B) 1878
    (C) 1876 (D) 1877
90. Broad System of Ordering (BSO)
    (A) 1978 (B) 1979
    (C) 1980 (D) 1981
91. DDC 22nd edition is published by
    (A) Forest Press (B) OCLC
    (C) IFLA (D) UNESCO.
92. Dewey Decimal Classification (DDC) is now looked after by?
    (A) UNESCO (B) CILIP
    (C) ALA (D) OCLC
93. The standard size of a catalogue card is
    (A) 12.5 cm X 7.5 cm (B) 12 cm X 7 cm
    (C) 11 cm X 5 cm (D) 10 cm X 4 cm
94. The Library of Congress Classification system divides human knowledge into
    (A) 20 major classes. (B) 21 major classes.
    (C) 25 major classes. (D) 30 major classes.
95. Riders International Classification
    (A) 1958 (B) 1959
    (C) 1960 (D) 1961
96. Paul Otlet and Henri La Fontaine related to
    (A) Sears List of Subject Heading
    (B) Library of Congress Classification System
    (C) UDC
    (D) Dictionary Catalogue

97. RDA related to
    (A) Classification (B) Cataloguing
    (C) Searching (D) Browsing

98. Dr. Nihar Ranjan Roy related to
    (A) Application of Ranganathan's Laws to the Web
    (B) The first professionally qualified university librarian in India
    (C) He for the first time in India, DDC and AACR rule introduced.
    (D) The first librarian of the Imperial Library (now National Library, Kolkata)

99. J. C. M. Hanson related to
    (A) Sears List of Subject Heading
    (B) Library of Congress Classification System
    (C) UDC
    (D) Dictionary Catalogue

100. Virtua accomadates Different version of the MARC Standard?
    (A) USMARC
    (B) UKMARC
    (C) CANMARC
    (D) SWEMARC/All of above

101. Expansive Classification (EC) invented in
    (A) 1881 (B) 1891
    (C) 1892 (D) 1893

102. OPAC stands for
    (A) Online Public Access Catalouge
    (B) Online Public Access Centre
    (C) Offline Public Acess Catalouge
    (B) Offline Public Access Centre

103. Which of the following are the salient features of UDC-IME?

(i) Minimum three digits in a class number
(ii) Main Class 4 is vacant
(iii) notation is independent of any particular language or script
(iv) more suitable for microdocuments

Codes :

(A) (i), (ii) and (iii) are correct
(B) (i), (ii) and (iv) are correct
(C) (ii), (iii) and (iv) are correct
(D) (i), (iii) and (iv) are correct

104. Who is the Editor in Chief of 19th Edition of DDC
(A) Benjamin A. Custer (B) John P. Comaromi
(C) Winton E. Matthews (D) John S. Mitchell

105. DDC classifies knowledge into ________ main subject groups
(A) 10 (B) 100
(C) 999 (D) 1000

106. Which editions of DDC is published by OCLC
(A) Abridged (B) Unabridged
(C) Both (D) None of the above

107. Unabridged version of DDC consist of ______ volumes
(A) Single (B) Two
(C) Three (D) Four

108. The latest edition of Unabridged DDC print version is
(A) 21st (B) 22nd
(C) 23rd (D) 24th

109. Unabridged version of DDC published aproximately every
(A) Six years (B) Seven years
(C) Eight years (D) Ten years

110. Abridged edition 15 is the latest Abridged edition of DDC published in

(A) Feb 2011 (B) Feb 2012
(C) Feb 2013 (D) Feb 2014

111. _______is a version of DDC intended to be used by libraries with in-depth religious collections and small general collections
(A) 50 Religion Class (B) 100 Religion Class
(C) 150 Religion Class (D) 200 Religion Class

112. The Index of DDC is called is called Relative index. In the Relative Index subjects are arrange
(A) Alphabetically (B) Chronologically
(C) Hierarchically (D) All the above

113. Universal Decimal Classification developed by Henri La Fontaine and Paul Otlet in
(A) 1901 (B) 1902
(C) 1903 (D) 1904

114. UDC based on
(A) Subject Classification
(B) Colon Classification
(C) Dewey Decimal Classification
(D) Expansive classification

115. UDC first published in which language?
(A) Belgium (B) English
(C) French (D) German

116. UDC schedules in the electronic format called
(A) UDC Master Reference File
(B) UDCC online
(C) UDC Online
(D) UDC Schedule online

117. UDC print version consists of
(A) Single Volume (B) 2 Volumes
(C) 3 Volumes (D) 4 Volumes

118. UDC regularly updated and maintained by

(A) FID (B) IFLA
(C) BIS (D) UDCC

119. Universal Decimal Classification is a/an
    (A) Enumarative Scheme
    (B) Almost faceted Scheme
    (C) Faceted Scheme
    (D) Rigidly Faceted
120. In UDC, Universe of knowledge divided into
    (A) 9 main classes (B) 5 main classes
    (C) 10 main classes (D) 100
121. Which is not a merit of Universal classification
    (i) expansive and adaptive quality of notation
    (ii) updates and degree of support
    (iii) highly flexible and effective
    (iv) Enumarative scheme
    (A) 1 only (B) 2 only
    (C) 3 only (D) 4 only
122. When UDC ownership transferred from FID to UDCC?
    (A) 1992 (B) 2002
    (C) 2012 (D) 2014
123. Which one of the following is example for Enumerative Classification
    (A) Riders International Classification
    (B) Dewey Decimal Classification
    (C) Universal Decimal Classification
    (D) Colon classification
124. Which one of the following is example for Almost Enumerative Classification
    (A) Riders International Classification
    (B) Dewey Decimal Classification
    (C) Universal Decimal Classification
    (D) Colon classification Ed.1

125. Which one of the following is example for Almost faceted Classification
   (A) Riders International Classification
   (B) Dewey Decimal Classification
   (C) Universal Decimal Classification
   (D) Colon classification Ed.2
126. Which one of the following is example for Rigidly Faceted Classification
   (A) Universal Decimal Classification
   (B) Dewey Decimal Classification
   (C) Colon classification Ed.1
   (D) Colon classification Ed.4
127. Which one of the following is example for Almost Freely Faceted Classification
   (A) Universal Decimal Classification
   (B) Dewey Decimal Classification
   (C) Colon classification Ed.5
   (D) Colon classification Ed.7
128. Which one of the following is example for Fully Freely Faceted Classification
   (A) Riders International Classification
   (B) Dewey Decimal Classification
   (C) Colon classification Ed.1
   (D) Colon classification Ed.7
129. DDC first published in 1876 with _______Pages.
   (A) 12 (B) 44
   (C) 72 (D) 84
130. The first english edition of UDC published in
   (A) 1904 (B) 1924
   (C) 1936 (D) 1942
131. In UDC, Common auxiliaries of Race & Nationality represented as

(A) (=) (B) ("")
(C) (1/9) (D) (.00)

132. In UDC, Common auxiliaries of Time represented as
(A) (=) (B) ("")
(C) (1/9) (D) (.00)

133. The word 'catalogue' has been derived from the ______ 'kata logos'.
(A) Latin (B) Greek
(C) Spanish (D) German

134. Which of the following is not a type of entry in a dictionary catalogue are
(a) Main Entry, (b) Collaborator Entry,
(c) Subject Entry, (d) Title Entry,
(e) Cross Reference Entries.
(A) (b) (B) (c)
(C) (e) (D) None

135. Which of the following constitutes the body of the main entry
1. Title and Statement of responsibility
2. Call Number
3. Material or type of Publication
4. Publication, distribution etc,
(A) 1, 2, 3 (B) 2, 3, 4
(C) 1, 3, 4 (D) 1, 2, 3, 4

136. Which of the following is not a type of entry in a classified catalogue are
(a) Main Entry,
(b) Cross Reference Entries,
(c) Class Index Entries,
(d) Book Index Entries,
(e) Cross Reference Index Entries.
(A) (e) (B) (d)
(C) (c) (D) None

137. Which one of the following is not in the three types of analytical entries in the Classified Catalogue Code
(a) Author Analyticals
(b) Title Analyticals
(c) Collaborator Analyticals
(d) Subject Analyticals
(A) (a) (B) (b)
(C) (c) (D) (d)

138. MARC Stands For
(A) Machine Readable Catalogue
(B) Machine Readable Cataloguing
(C) Machine Readable Class Number
(D) Machine Access and Readable Catalogue

139. In MARC 110 Represents
(A) Meeting Name (B) Publisher Information
(C) Personnel Name (D) Corporate Name

140. In MARC 260 Represents
(A) Physical Description
(B) ISBN
(C) Personnel Name
(D) Publisher Information

141. In MARC 250 Represents
(A) Edition Statements (B) Title Statements
(C) Personnel Name (D) Corporate Name

142. In MARC 020 Represents
(A) Edition Statements (B) ISBN
(C) Personnel Name (D) Corporate Name

143. In MARC 852 Represents
(A) Uniform Title (B) Location
(C) Personnel Name (D) Title Statement

144. In MARC 648 Represents
(A) Chronological Term (B) Topical Term
(C) Corporate Name (D) Uniform Name

145. In MARC 130 Represents
(A) Chronology Term (B) Topical Term
(C) Corporate Name (D) Uniform Name

146. In MARC 245 Represents
(A) Edition Statements (B) Title Statements
(C) Personnel Name (D) Corporate Name

147. In MARC 6xx Represents
(A) Edition Statements (B) Subject Added Entry
(C) Personnel Name (D) Corporate Name

148. In DDC Main Class Number 400 used for
(A) Language (B) Science
(C) Philosophy (D) Computer

149. In DDC Main Class Number 330 used for
(A) Physics (B) Economics
(C) Library Science (D) Electronics

150. In DDC Main Class Number 658 used for
(A) Marketing (B) Advertising
(C) General Management(D) Geography

ANSWERS

1 (B)	2 (C)	3 (A)	4 (C)	5 (A)	6 (A)
7 (A)	8 (D)	9 (B)	10 (B)	11 (A)	12 (A)
13 (B)	14 (B)	15 (B)	16 (A)	17 (B)	18 (A)
19 (B)	20 (A)	21 (A)	22 (B)	23 (D)	24 (D)
25 (A)	26 (B)	27 (C)	28 (D)	29 (C)	30 (B)
31 (B)	32 (A)	33 (C)	34 (B)	35 (B)	36 (A)
37 (A)	38 (A)	39 (A)	40 (A)	41 (B)	42 (D)
43 (A)	44 (A)	45 (C)	46 (B)	47 (A)	48 (B)
49 (B)	50 (C)	51 (C)	52 (B)	53 (A)	54 (B)
55 (C)	56 (B)	57 (D)	58 (B)	59 (A)	60 (B)
61 (C)	62 (C)	63 (C)	64 (B)	65 (D)	66 (A)
67 (D)	68 (B)	69 (B)	70 (A)	71 (A)	72 (C)
73 (B)	74 (B)	75 (C)	76 (D)	77 (C)	78 (D)
79 (C)	80 (B)	81 (D)	82 (C)	83 (D)	84 (A)
85 (A)	86 (A)	87 (A)	88 (D)	89 (C)	90 (A)
91 (B)	92 (D)	93 (A)	94 (B)	95 (D)	96 (C)
97 (B)	98 (C)	99 (B)	100 (D)	101 (B)	102 (A)
103 (D)	104 (A)	105 (A)	106 (C)	107 (D)	108 (C)
109 (B)	110 (B)	111 (D)	112 (A)	113 (D)	114 (C)
115 (C)	116 (A)	117 (B)	118 (D)	119 (B)	120 (C)
121 (D)	122 (A)	123 (A)	124 (B)	125 (C)	126 (C)
127 (C)	128 (D)	129 (B)	130 (C)	131 (A)	132 (B)
133 (B)	134 (D)	135 (C)	136 (D)	137 (C)	138 (B)
139 (D)	140 (D)	141 (A)	142 (B)	143 (B)	144 (A)
145 (D)	146 (B)	147 (B)	148 (A)	149 (B)	150 (C)

Dewey Decimal Classification Main classes (DDC)

Sr. No	*Class Number*	*Class Subject*
1	000	Computer Science, Information & General Works
2	100	Philosophy & Psychology
3	200	Religion
4	300	Social Science
5	400	Language
6	500	Science
7	600	Technology
8	700	Arts & Recreation
9	800	Literature
10	900	History & Geography

LIST OF DEWEY DECIMAL MAIN CLASSES

000 Computer science, knowledge & systems

000 Computer science, information & general works

001 Knowledge

002 The book (writing, libraries, and book related topics)

003 Systems

004 Data processing & computer science

005 Computer programming, programs & data

006 Special computer methods

007-009

010 Bibliographies

010 Bibliography

011 Bibliographies

012 Bibliographies of individuals
013 [Unassigned]
014 Bibliographies of anonymous & pseudonymous works
015 Bibliographies of works from specific places
016 Bibliographies of works on specific subjects
017 General subject catalogs
018 Catalogs arranged by author, date, etc.
019 Dictionary catalogs
020 Library & information sciences
020 Library & information sciences
021 Library relationships (with archives, information centers, etc.)
022 Administration of physical plant
023 Personnel management
024 [Unassigned]
025 Library operations
026 Libraries for specific subjects
027 General libraries
028 Reading & use of other information media
029 [Unassigned]
030 Encyclopedias & books of facts
030 General encyclopedic works
031 Encyclopedias in American English
032 Encyclopedias in English
033 Encyclopedias in other Germanic languages
034 Encyclopedias in French, Occitan, and Catalan
035 Encyclopedias in Italian, Romanian, and related languages
036 Encyclopedias in Spanish & Portuguese
037 Encyclopedias in Slavic languages
038 Encyclopedias in Scandinavian languages
039 Encyclopedias in other languages

040 Unassigned ***(formerly Biographies)***

050 Magazines, journals & serials

050 General serial publications
051 Serials in American English
052 Serials in English
053 Serials in other Germanic languages
054 Serials in French, Occitan, and Catalan
055 Serials in Italian, Romanian, and related languages
056 Serials in Spanish & Portuguese
057 Serials in Slavic languages
058 Serials in Scandinavian languages
059 Serials in other languages

060 Associations, organizations & museums

060 General organizations & museum science
061 Organizations in North America
062 Organizations in British Isles; in England
063 Organizations in central Europe; in Germany
064 Organizations in France & Monaco
065 Organizations in Italy & adjacent islands
066 Organizations in Iberian peninsula & adjacent islands
067 Organizations in eastern Europe; in Russia
068 Organizations in other geographic areas
069 Museum science

070 News media, journalism & publishing

070 News media, journalism, and publishing
071 Newspapers in North America
072 Newspapers in British Isles; in England
073 Newspapers in central Europe; in Germany
074 Newspapers in France & Monaco
075 Newspapers in Italy & adjacent islands
076 Newspapers in Iberian peninsula & adjacent islands
077 Newspapers in eastern Europe; in Russia

078 Newspapers in Scandinavia
079 Newspapers in other geographic areas
080 Quotations
080 General collections
081 Collections in American English
082 Collections in English
083 Collections in other Germanic languages
084 Collections in French, Occitan, Catalan
085 Collections in Italian, Romanian, & related languages
086 Collections in Spanish & Portuguese
087 Collections in Slavic languages
088 Collections in Scandinavian languages
089 Collections in other languages
090 Manuscripts & rare books
090 Manuscripts and rare books
091 Manuscripts
092 Block books
093 Incunabula
094 Printed books
095 Books notable for bindings
096 Books notable for illustrations
097 Books notable for ownership or origin
098 Prohibited works, forgeries, and hoaxes
099 Books notable for format
100 Philosophy
100 Philosophy & psychology
101 Theory of philosophy
102 Miscellany
103 Dictionaries & encyclopedias
104 [Unassigned]
105 Serial publications
106 Organizations & management

107 Education, research, related topics of philosophy
108 Groups of people
109 History & collected biography
110 Metaphysics
110 Metaphysics
111 Ontology
112 *No longer used – formerly Methodology*
113 Cosmology (Philosophy of nature)
114 Space
115 Time
116 Change
117 Structure
118 Force and energy
119 Number and quantity
120 Epistemology
120 Epistemology, causation, and humankind
121 Epistemology (Theory of knowledge)
122 Causation
123 Determinism and indeterminism
124 Teleology
125 *No longer used – formerly Infinity*
126 The self
127 The unconscious & the subconscious
128 Humankind
129 Origin & destiny of individual souls
130 Parapsychology & occultism
130 Parapsychology & occultism
131 Parapsychological and occult methods for achieving well-being, happiness, success
132 *No longer used – formerly Mental derangements*
133 Specific topics in parapsychology & occultism
134 *No longer used – formerly Mesmerism & Clairvoyance*

135 Dreams & mysteries
136 *No longer used – formerly Mental characteristics*
137 Divinatory graphology
138 Physiognomy
139 Phrenology

140 Philosophical schools of thought

140 Specific philosophical schools and viewpoints
141 Idealism & related systems & doctrines
142 Critical philosophy
143 Bergsonism & intuitionism
144 Humanism & related systems & doctrines
145 Sensationalism
146 Naturalism & related systems & doctrines
147 Pantheism & related systems & doctrines
148 Dogmatism, eclecticism, liberalism, syncretism, & traditionalism
149 Other philosophical systems & doctrines

150 Psychology

150 Psychology
151 *No longer used – formerly Intellect*
152 Sensory perception, movement, emotions, & physiological drives
153 Conscious mental processes & intelligence
154 Subconscious & altered states & processes
155 Differential & developmental psychology
156 Comparative psychology
157 *No longer used – formerly Emotions*
158 Applied psychology
159 *No longer used – formerly Will*

160 Philosophical logic

160 Philosophical logic
161 Induction

162 Deduction
163-164 *Not assigned or no longer used*
165 Fallacies & sources of error
166 Syllogisms
167 Hypotheses
168 Argument & persuasion
169 Analogy
170 Ethics
170 Ethics (Moral philosophy)
171 Ethical systems
172 Political ethics
173 Ethics of family relationships
174 Occupational ethics
175 Ethics of recreation, leisure, public performances, communication
176 Ethics of sex & reproduction
177 Ethics of social relations
178 Ethics of consumption
179 Other ethical norms
180 Ancient, medieval, & Eastern philosophy
180 Ancient, medieval, eastern philosophy
181 Eastern philosophy
182 Pre-Socratic Greek philosophies
183 Sophistic, Socratic, related Greek philosophies
184 Platonic philosophy
185 Aristotelian philosophy
186 Skeptic & Neoplatonic philosophies
187 Epicurean philosophy
188 Stoic philosophy
189 Medieval Western philosophy
190 Modern Western philosophy (19th-century, 20th-century)

190 Modern Western & other noneastern philosophy
191 Philosophy of the United States and Canada
192 Philosophy of the British Isles
193 Philosophy of Germany and Austria
194 Philosophy of France
195 Philosophy of Italy
196 Philosophy of Spain and Portugal
197 Philosophy of Russia
198 Philosophy of Scandinavia & Finland
199 Philosophy in other geographic areas

200 Religion

200 Religion
201 Religious mythology, general classes of religion, interreligious relations and attitudes, social theology
202 Doctrines
203 Public worship and other practices
204 Religious experience, life, practice
205 Religious ethics
206 Leaders and organization
207 Missions and religious education
208 Sources
209 Sects and reform movements

210 Philosophy & theory of religion

210 Philosophy & theory of religion
211 Concepts of God
212 Existence, ways of knowing God, attributes of God
213 Creation
214 Theodicy
215 Science & religion
216 *No longer used – formerly Evil*
217 *No longer used – formerly Prayer*
218 Humankind

219 *No longer used – formerly Analogies*

220 The Bible

220 Bible

221 Old Testament (Tanakh)

222 Historical books of Old Testament

223 Poetic books of Old Testament

224 Prophetic books of Old Testament

225 New Testament

226 Gospels & Acts

227 Epistles

228 Revelation (Apocalypse)

229 Apocrypha, pseudepigrapha, & intertestamental works

230 Christianity

230 Christianity

231 God

232 Jesus Christ & his family

233 Humankind

234 Salvation & grace

235 Spiritual beings

236 Eschatology

237 *No longer used – formerly Future state*

238 Creeds, confessions of faith, covenants, & catechisms

239 Apologetics & polemics

240 Christian practice & observance

240 Christian moral and devotional theology

241 Christian ethics

242 Devotional literature

243 Evangelistic writings for individuals and families

244 *No longer used – formerly Religious fiction*

245 *No longer used – formerly Hymnology*

246 Use of art in Christianity

247 Church furnishings & related articles

248 Christian experience, practice, life

249 Christian observances in family life

250 Christian orders & local church

250 Local Christian church and Christian religious orders

251 Preaching (Homiletics)

252 Texts of sermons

253 Pastoral office and work (Pastoral theology)

254 Parish administration

255 Religious congregations & orders

256 *No longer used – formerly Religious societies*

257 *No longer used – formerly Parochial schools, libraries, etc.*

258 *No longer used – formerly Parochial medicine*

259 Pastoral care of families, of specific groups of people

260 Social & ecclesiastical theology

260 Christian social and ecclesiastical theology

261 Social theology and interreligious relations and attitudes

262 Ecclesiology

263 Days, times, places of religious observance

264 Public worship

265 Sacraments, other rites & acts

266 Missions

267 Associations for religious work

268 Religious education

269 Spiritual renewal

270 History of Christianity

270 History, geographic treatment, biography of Christianity

271 Religious congregations and orders in church history

272 Persecutions in church history

[illegible]ical controversies and heresies in general church

274 Christianity in Europe
275 Christianity in Asia
276 Christianity in Africa
277 Christianity in North America
278 Christianity in South America
279 History of Christianity in other areas
280 Christian denominations
280 Denominations and sects of Christian church
281 Early church & Eastern churches
282 Roman Catholic Church
283 Anglican churches
284 Protestant denominations of Continental origin & related body
285 Presbyterian churches, Reformed churches centered in America, Congregational churches
286 Baptist, Restoration Movement, Adventist churches
287 Methodist churches; churches related to Methodism
288 *No longer used – formerly Unitarian*
289 Other denominations & sects
290 Other religions
290 Other religions
291 *No longer used – formerly Comparative religion*
292 Classical religion (Greek & Roman religion)
293 Germanic religion
294 Religions of Indic origin
295 Zoroastrianism (Mazdaism, Parseeism)
296 Judaism
297 Islam, Bábism & Bahá'í Faith
298 *No longer used – formerly Mormonism*
299 Religions not provided for elsewhere
300 Social sciences, sociology & anthropology
300 Social sciences

301 Sociology & anthropology
302 Social interaction
303 Social processes
304 Factors affecting social behavior
305 Groups of people
306 Culture & institutions
307 Communities
308 *No longer used – formerly Polygraphy*
309 *No longer used – formerly History of sociology*
310 Statistics
310 Collections of general statistics
311 *No longer used – formerly Theory and methods*
312 *No longer used – formerly Population*
313 *No longer used – formerly Special topics*
314 General statistics of Europe
315 General statistics of Asia
316 General statistics of Africa
317 General statistics of North America
318 General statistics of South America
319 General statistics of Australasia, Pacific Ocean islands, Atlantic Ocean islands, Arctic islands, Antarctica
320 Political science
320 Political science (Politics & government)
321 Systems of governments & states
322 Relation of state to organized groups & their members
323 Civil & political rights
324 The political process
325 International migration & colonization
326 Slavery & emancipation
327 International relations
328 The legislative process
329 *Not assigned or no longer used*

330 Economics

330 Economics

331 Labor economics

332 Financial economics

333 Economics of land & energy

334 Cooperatives

335 Socialism & related systems

336 Public finance

337 International economics

338 Production

339 Macroeconomics & related topics

340 Law

340 Law

341 Law of nations

342 Constitutional & administrative law

343 Military, defense, public property, public finance, tax, commerce (trade), industrial law

344 Labor, social service, education, cultural law

345 Criminal law

346 Private law

347 Procedure & courts

348 Laws, regulations, cases

349 Law of specific jurisdictions, areas, socioeconomic regions, regional intergovernmental organizations

350 Public administration & military science

350 Public administration & military science

351 Public administration

352 General considerations of public administration

353 Specific fields of public administration

354 Public administration of economy & environment

355 Military science

356 Foot forces & warfare

357 Mounted forces & warfare
358 Air & other specialized forces & warfare; engineering & related services
359 Sea forces & warfare
360 Social problems & social services
360 Social problems & services; associations
361 Social problems & services
362 Social problems of & services to groups of people
363 Other social problems & services
364 Criminology
365 Penal & related institutions
366 Secret associations & societies
367 General clubs
368 Insurance
369 Associations
370 Education
370 Education
371 Schools & their activities; special education
372 Primary education (elementary education)
373 Secondary education
374 Adult education
375 Curricula
376 *No longer used – formerly Education of women*
377 *No longer used – formerly Ethical education*
378 Higher education (Tertiary education)
379 Public policy issues in education
380 Commerce, communications, & transportation
380 Commerce, communications, transportation
381 Commerce (Trade)
382 International commerce (Foreign trade)
383 Postal communication
384 Communications

385 Railroad transportation
386 Inland waterway & ferry transportation
387 Water, air, space transportation
388 Transportation
389 Metrology & standardization
390 Customs, etiquette, & folklore
390 Customs, etiquette, folklore
391 Costume & personal appearance
392 Customs of life cycle & domestic life
393 Death customs
394 General customs
395 Etiquette (Manners)
396 *No longer used – formerly Women's position and treatment*
397 *No longer used – formerly outcast studies*
398 Folklore
399 Customs of war & diplomacy
400 Language
400 Language
401 Philosophy & theory; international languages
402 Miscellany
403 Dictionaries, encyclopedias, concordances
404 Special topics of language
405 Serial publications
406 Organizations & management
407 Education, research, related topics
408 Groups of people
409 Geographic treatment & biography
410 Linguistics
410 Linguistics
411 Writing systems of standard forms of languages
412 Etymology of standard forms of languages
413 Dictionaries of standard forms of languages

414 Phonology & phonetics of standard forms of languages
415 Grammar of standard forms of languages
416 *No longer used – formerly Prosody*
417 Dialectology & historical linguistics
418 Standard usage (Prescriptive linguistics)
419 Sign languages
420 English & Old English languages
420 English & Old English (Anglo-Saxon)
421 Writing system, phonology, phonetics of standard English
422 Etymology of standard English
423 Dictionaries of standard English
424 *No longer used – formerly English thesauruses*
425 Grammar of standard English
426 *No longer used – formerly English prosodies*
427 Historical & geographical variations, modern nongeographic variations of English
428 Standard English usage (Prescriptive linguistics)
429 Old English (Anglo-Saxon)
430 German & related languages
430 German and related languages
431 Writing systems, phonology, phonetics of standard German
432 Etymology of standard German
433 Dictionaries of standard German
434 *Not assigned or no longer used*
435 Grammar of standard German
436 *Not assigned or no longer used*
437 Historical & geographic variations, modern nongeographic variations of German
438 Standard German usage (Prescriptive linguistics)
439 Other Germanic languages

440 French & related languages

440 French & related Romance languages

441 Writing systems, phonology, phonetics of standard French

442 Etymology of standard French

443 Dictionaries of standard French

444 *Not assigned or no longer used*

445 Grammar of standard French

446 *Not assigned or no longer used*

447 Historical and geographic variations, modern nongeographic variations of French

448 Standard French usage (Prescriptive linguistics)

449 Occitan Catalan, Franco-Provençal

450 Italian, Romanian, & related languages

450 Italian, Dalmatian, Romanian, Rhaetian, Sardinian, Corsican

451 Writing systems, phonology, phonetics of standard Italian

452 Etymology of standard Italian

453 Dictionaries of standard Italian

454 *Not assigned or no longer used*

455 Grammar of standard Italian

456 *Not assigned or no longer used*

457 Historical & geographic variations, modern nongeographic variations of Italian

458 Standard Italian usage (Prescriptive linguistics)

459 Romanian, Rhaetian, Sardinian, Corsican

460 Spanish, Portuguese, Galician

460 Spanish, Portuguese, Galician

461 Writing systems, phonology, phonetics of standard Spanish

462 Etymology of standard Spanish

463 Dictionaries of standard Spanish
464 *Not assigned or no longer used*
465 Grammar of standard Spanish
466 *Not assigned or no longer used*
467 Historical & geographic variations, modern nongeographic variations of Spanish
468 Standard Spanish usage (Prescriptive linguistics)
469 Portuguese
470 Latin & Italic languages
470 Latin & related Italic languages
471 Writing systems, phonology, phonetics of classical Latin
472 Etymology of classical Latin
473 Dictionaries of classical Latin
474 *Not assigned or no longer used*
475 Grammar of classical Latin
476 *Not assigned or no longer used*
477 Old, postclassical, Vulgar Latin
478 Classical Latin usage (Prescriptive linguistics)
479 Other Italic languages
480 Classical & modern Greek languages
480 Classical Greek & related Hellenic languages
481 Writing systems, phonology, phonetics of classical Greek
482 Etymology of classical Greek
483 Dictionaries of classical Greek
484 *Not assigned or no longer used*
485 Grammar of classical Greek
486 *Not assigned or no longer used*
487 Preclassical & postclassical Greek
488 Classical Greek usage (Prescriptive linguistics)
489 Other Hellenic languages

490 Other languages

490 Other languages
491 East Indo-European & Celtic languages
492 Afro-Asiatic languages
493 Non-Semitic Afro-Asiatic languages
494 Altic, Uralic, Hyperborean, Dravidian languages, miscellaneous languages of south Asia
495 Languages of East & Southeast Asia
496 African languages
497 North American native languages
498 South American native languages
499 Non-Austronesian languages of Oceania, Austronesian languages, miscellaneous languages

500 Science

500 Natural sciences & mathematics
501 Philosophy & theory
502 Miscellany
503 Dictionaries, encyclopedias, concordances
504 *Not assigned or no longer used*
505 Serial publications
506 Organizations & management
507 Education, research, related topics
508 Natural history
509 History, geographic treatment, biography

510 Mathematics

510 Mathematics
511 General principles of mathematics
512 Algebra
513 Arithmetic
514 Topology
515 Analysis
516 Geometry

517 *Not assigned or no longer used*
518 Numerical analysis
519 Probabilities & applied mathematics
520 Astronomy
520 Astronomy & allied sciences
521 Celestial mechanics
522 Techniques, procedures, apparatus, equipment, materials
523 Specific celestial bodies & phenomena
524 *Not assigned or no longer used*
525 Earth (Astronomical geography)
526 Mathematical geography
527 Celestial navigation
528 Ephemerides
529 Chronology
530 Physics
530 Physics
531 Classical mechanics
532 Fluid mechanics
533 Pneumatics (Gas mechanics)
534 Sound & related vibrations
535 Light & related radiation
536 Heat
537 Electricity & electronics
538 Magnetism
539 Modern physics
540 Chemistry
540 Chemistry & allied sciences
541 Physical chemistry
542 Techniques, procedures, apparatus, equipment, materials
543 Analytical chemistry

544 *No longer used-formerly Qualitative analysis*
545 *No longer used-formerly Quantitative analysis*
546 Inorganic chemistry
547 Organic chemistry
548 Crystallography
549 Mineralogy
550 Earth sciences & geology
550 Earth sciences
551 Geology, hydrology, meteorology
552 Petrology
553 Economic geology
554 Earth sciences of Europe
555 Earth sciences of Asia
556 Earth sciences of Africa
557 Earth sciences of North America
558 Earth sciences of South America
559 Earth sciences of Australasia, Pacific Ocean islands, Atlantic Ocean islands, Arctic islands, Antarctica, extraterrestrial worlds
560 Fossils & prehistoric life
560 Paleontology
561 Paleobotany; fossil microorganisms
562 Fossil invertebrates
563 Miscellaneous fossil marine & seashore invertebrates
564 Fossil Mollusca & Molluscoidea
565 Fossil Arthropoda
566 Fossil Chordata
567 Fossil cold-blooded vertebrates
568 Fossil Aves (birds)
569 Fossil Mammalia
570 Biology
570 Biology

571 Physiology & related subjects
572 Biochemistry
573 Specific physiological systems in animals, regional histology & physiology in animals
574 *Not assigned or no longer used*
575 Specific parts of & physiological systems in plants
576 Genetics and evolution
577 Ecology
578 Natural history of organisms & related subjects
579 Natural history of microorganisms, fungi, algae

580 Plants

580 Plants
581 Specific topics in natural history of plants
582 Plants noted for specific vegetative characteristics and flowers
583 Magnoliopsida (Dicotyledones)
584 Liliopsida (Monocotyledones)
585 Pinophyta (Gymnosperms)
586 Cryptogamia (Seedless plants)
587 Pteridophyta
588 Bryophyta
589 *No longer used-formerly Forestry*

590 Animals (Zoology)

590 Animals
591 Specific topics in natural history of animals
592 Invertebrates
593 Miscellaneous marine & seashore invertebrates
594 Mollusca & Molluscoidea
595 Arthropoda
596 Chordata
597 Cold-blooded vertebrates
598 Aves (Birds)

599 Mammalia (Mammals)

600 Technology

600 Technology (Applied sciences)

601 Philosophy & theory

602 Miscellany

603 Dictionaries, encyclopedias, concordances

604 Technical drawing, hazardous materials technology; groups of people

605 Serial publications

606 Organizations

607 Education, research, related topics

608 Patents

609 History, geographic treatment, biography

610 Medicine & health

610 Medicine & health

- 610.3 Medical encyclopedias
- 610.6 Medical organizations & professions
- 610.72 Medical research
- 610.9 Geography and history of medicine

611 Human anatomy, cytology, histology

- 611.2 Respiratory (lung, respiratory system)
- 611.3 Gastrointestinal (dental anatomy)
- 611.6 Genitourinary (genital system)
- 611.7 Musculoskeletal (seed coat)
- 611.8 Anatomy of the sense organs and nervous system
- 611.82 Anatomy of the brain
- 611.9 Topographic anatomy (back)

612 Human physiology

613 Personal health & safety

- 613.023 Professions hygiene and health
- 613.1 Role of the natural environment

613.2 Diet (food hygiene, nutrition, diet, nutritional value of food and beverages)

613.4 Cleanliness Care (hygiene and personal cleanliness, personal care)

613.5 Role of unnatural environment (housing, housing, temperature)

613.6

613.62 Hygiene in the business (industrial hygiene)

613.66 Self Defense

613.7 Condition physique (bodybuilding, fitness, forme physique)

613.7046 Hatha yoga, yoga physique

613.71 Exercising, sports (aerobics, sauna, appearance surveillance and physical form)

613.79 Relaxation, sleep

614 Forensic medicine; incidence of injuries, wounds, disease; public preventive medicine

615 Pharmacology and therapeutics

616 Diseases

617 Surgery, regional medicine, dentistry, ophthalmology, otology, audiology

618 Gynecology, obstetrics, pediatrics, geriatrics

619 *No longer used-formerly Experimental medicine*

620 Engineering

620 Engineering & Applied operations

621 Applied physics

622 Mining & related operations

623 Military & nautical engineering

624 Civil engineering

625 Engineering of railroads, roads

626 *Not assigned or no longer used*

627 Hydraulic engineering
628 Sanitary engineering
629 Other branches of engineering
630 Agriculture
630 Agriculture & related technologies
631 Specific techniques; apparatus, equipment, materials
632 Plant injuries, diseases, pests
633 Field & plantation crops
634 Orchards, fruits, forestry
635 Garden crops (Horticulture)
636 Animal husbandry
637 Processing dairy & related products
638 Insect culture
639 Hunting, fishing, conservation, related technologies
640 Home & family management
640 Home & family management
641 Food & drink
642 Meals & table service
643 Housing & household equipment
644 Household utilities
645 Household furnishings
646 Sewing, clothing, management of personal and family life
647 Management of public households (Institutional housekeeping)
648 Housekeeping
649 Child rearing; home care of people with disabilities & illnesses
650 Management & public relations
650 Management & auxiliary services
651 Office services
652 Processes of written communication

653 Shorthand

654-656 *Not assigned or no longer used*

657 Accounting

658 General management

659 Advertising & public relations

660 Chemical engineering

660 Chemical engineering & related technologies

661 Technology of industrial chemicals

662 Technology of explosives, fuels, related products

663 Beverage technology

664 Food technology

665 Technology of industrial oils, fats, waxes, gases

666 Ceramic & allied technologies

667 Cleaning, color, coating, related technologies

668 Technology of other organic products

669 Metallurgy

670 Manufacturing

670 Manufacturing

671 Metalworking processes & primary metal products

672 Iron, steel, other iron alloys

673 Nonferrous metals

674 Lumber processing, wood products, cork

675 Leather & fur processing

676 Pulp & paper technology

677 Textiles

678 Elastomers & elastomer products

679 Other products of specific kinds of materials

680 Manufacture for specific uses

680 Manufacture of products for specific uses

681 Precision instruments & other devices

682 Small forge work (Blacksmithing)

683 Hardware & household appliances

684 Furnishings & home workshops
685 Leather & fur goods, & related products
686 Printing & related activities
687 Clothing & accessories
688 Other final products, & packaging technology
689 *Not assigned or no longer used*
690 Construction of buildings
690 Construction of buildings
691 Building materials
692 Auxiliary construction practices
693 Construction in specific types of materials & for specific purposes
694 Wood construction
695 Roof covering
696 Utilities
697 Heating, ventilating, air-conditioning engineering
698 Detail finishing
699 *Not assigned or no longer used*
700 Arts
700 The Arts
701 Philosophy & theory of fine & decorative arts
702 Miscellany of fine & decorative arts
703 Dictionaries, encyclopedias, concordances of fine & decorative arts
704 Special topics in fine & decorative arts
705 Serial publications of fine & decorative arts
706 Organizations & management of fine & decorative arts
707 Education, research, related topics of fine & decorative arts
708 Galleries, museums, private collections of fine & decorative arts
709 History, geographic treatment, biography

710 Area planning & landscape architecture

710 Area planning & landscape architecture
711 Area planning (Civic art)
712 Landscape architecture (Landscape design)
713 Landscape architecture of trafficways
714 Water features in landscape architecture
715 Woody plants in landscape architecture
716 Herbaceous plants in landscape architecture
717 Structures in landscape architecture
718 Landscape design of cemeteries
719 Natural landscapes

720 Architecture

720 Architecture
721 Architectural materials & structural elements
722 Architecture from earliest times to ca. 300
723 Architecture from ca. 300 to 1399
724 Architecture from 1400
725 Public structures
726 Buildings for religious & related purposes
727 Buildings for educational & research purposes
728 Residential & related buildings
729 Design & decoration of structures & accessories

730 Sculpture, ceramics, & metalwork

730 Sculpture & related arts
731 Processes, forms, subjects of sculpture
732 Sculpture from earliest times to ca. 500, sculpture of nonliterate peoples
733 Greek, Etruscan, Roman sculpture
734 Sculpture from ca. 500 to 1399
735 Sculpture from 1400
736 Carving & carvings
737 Numismatics & sigillography

738 Ceramic arts
739 Art metalwork
740 Graphic arts & decorative arts
740 Graphic arts
741 Drawing & drawings
742 Perspective in drawing
743 Drawing & drawings by subject
744 *Not assigned or no longer used*
745 Decorative arts
746 Textile arts
747 Interior decoration
748 Glass
749 Furniture & accessories
750 Painting
750 Painting & paintings
751 Techniques, procedures, apparatus, equipment, materials, forms
752 Color
753 Symbolism, allegory, mythology, legend
754 Genre paintings
755 Religion
756 *Not assigned or no longer used*
757 Human figures
758 Nature, architectural subjects & cityscapes, other specific subjects
759 History, geographic treatment, biography
760 Printmaking & prints
760 Printmaking & prints
761 Relief processes (Block printing)
762 *Not assigned or no longer used*
763 Lithographic processes (Planographic processes)
764 Chromolithography & serigraphy

765 Metal engraving

766 Mezzotinting, aquatinting, & related processes

767 Etching & drypoint

768 *Not assigned or no longer used*

769 Prints

770 Photography, computer art, film, video

770 Photography, computer art, cinematography, videography

771 Techniques, procedures, apparatus, equipment, materials

772 Metallic salt processes

773 Pigment processes of printing

774 *No longer used-formerly Holography*

775 *No longer used-formerly Digital photography*

776 Computer art (Digital art)

777 Cinematography & Videography

778 Specific fields & special kinds of photography

779 Photographic images

780 Music

780 Music

781 General principles & musical forms

782 Vocal music

783 Music for single voices

784 Instruments & Instrumental ensembles & their music

785 Ensembles with only one instrument per part

786 Keyboard, mechanical, electrophonic, percussion instruments

787 Stringed instruments (Chordophones)

788 Wind instruments (Aerophones)

789 *Not assigned or no longer used*

790 Sports, games & entertainment

790 Recreational & performing arts

791 Public performances
792 Stage presentations
793 Indoor games & amusements
794 Indoor games of skill
795 Games of chance
796 Athletic & outdoor sports & games
797 Aquatic & air sports
798 Equestrian sports & animal racing
799 Fishing, hunting, shooting
800 Literature, rhetoric & criticism
800 Literature (Belles-lettres) & rhetoric
801 Philosophy & theory
802 Miscellany
803 Dictionaries, encyclopedias, concordances
804 *Not assigned or no longer used*
805 Serial publications
806 Organizations & management
807 Education, research, related topics
808 Rhetoric & collections of literary texts from more than two literatures
809 History, description, critical appraisal of more than two literatures
810 American literature in English
810 American literature in English
811 American poetry in English
812 American drama in English
813 American fiction in English
814 American essays in English
815 American speeches in English
816 American letters in English
817 American humor & satire in English
818 American miscellaneous writings in English

819 *No longer used-formerly Puzzle activities*

820 English & Old English literatures

820 English & Old English (Anglo-Saxon) literatures

821 English Poetry

822 English drama

823 English fiction

824 English essays

825 English speeches

826 English letters

827 English humor & satire

828 English miscellaneous writings

829 Old English (Anglo-Saxon) literature

830 German & related literatures

830 German literature & literatures of related languages

831 German poetry

832 German drama

833 German fiction

834 German essays

835 German speeches

836 German letters

837 German humor & satire

838 German miscellaneous writings

839 Other Germanic literatures

840 French & related literatures

840 French literature & literatures of related Romance languages

841 French poetry

842 French drama

843 French fiction

844 French essays

845 French speeches

846 French letters

847 French humor & satire
848 French miscellaneous writings
849 Occitan, Catalan, Franco-Provençal literatures
850 Italian, Romanian, & related literatures
850 Literatures of Italian, Dalmatian, Romanian, Rhaetian, Sardinian, Corsican languages
851 Italian poetry
852 Italian drama
853 Italian fiction
854 Italian essays
855 Italian speeches
856 Italian letters
857 Italian humor & satire
858 Italian miscellaneous writings
859 Literatures of Romanian, Rhaetian, Sardinian, Corsican languages
860 Spanish, Portuguese, Galician literatures
860 Literatures of Spanish, Portuguese, Galician languages
861 Spanish poetry
862 Spanish drama
863 Spanish fiction
864 Spanish essays
865 Spanish speeches
866 Spanish letters
867 Spanish humor & satire
868 Spanish miscellaneous writings
869 Literatures of Portuguese & Galician languages
870 Latin & Italic literatures
870 Latin literature & literatures of related Italic languages
871 Latin poetry
872 Latin dramatic poetry & drama
873 Latin epic poetry & fiction

874 Latin lyric poetry
875 Latin speeches
876 Latin letters
877 Latin humor & satire
878 Latin miscellaneous writings
879 Literatures of other Italic languages
880 Classical & modern Greek literatures
880 Classical Greek literature & literatures of related Hellenic languages
881 Classical Greek poetry
882 Classical Greek drama
883 Classical Greek epic poetry & fiction
884 Classical Greek lyric poetry
885 Classical Greek speeches
886 Classical Greek letters
887 Classical Greek humor & satire
888 Classical Greek miscellaneous writings
889 Modern Greek literature
890 Other literatures
890 Literatures of other specific languages and language families
891 East Indo-European & Celtic literatures
892 Afro-Asiatic literatures
893 Non-Semitic Afro-Asiatic literatures
894 Literatures of Altaic, Uralic, Hyperborean, Dravidian languages; literatures of miscellaneous languages of Southeast Asia
895 Literatures of East & Southeast Asia
896 African literatures
897 Literatures of North American native languages
898 Literatures of South American native languages
899 Literatures of non-Austronesian languages of Oceania, of Austronesian languages, of miscellaneous languages

900 History

900 History, geography, & auxiliary disciplines
901 Philosophy & theory of history
902 Miscellany of history
903 Dictionaries, encyclopedias, concordances of history
904 Collected accounts of events
905 Serial publications of history
906 Organizations & management of history
907 Education, research, related topics of history
908 History with respect to groups of people
909 World history

910 Geography & travel

910 Geography & travel
911 Historical geography
912 Graphic representations of surface of earth and of extraterrestrial worlds
913 Geography of & travel in ancient world
914 Geography of & travel in Europe
915 Geography of & travel in Asia
916 Geography of & travel in Africa
917 Geography of & travel in North America
918 Geography of & travel in South America
919 Geography of & travel in Australasia, Pacific Ocean islands, Atlantic Ocean islands, Arctic islands, Antarctica, & on extraterrestrial worlds

920 Biography & genealogy

920 Biography, genealogy, insignia
921-928 This range is reserved as an optional location for biographies, which are shelved alphabetically by subject's last name.
929 Genealogy, names, insignia

930 History of ancient world (to ca. 499)

930 History of ancient world to ca. 499

931 China to 420
932 Egypt to 640
933 Palestine to 70
934 South Asia to 647
935 Mesopotamia to 637 & Iranian Plateau to 637
936 Europe north & west of Italian Peninsula to ca. 499
937 Italian Peninsula to 476 & adjacent territories to 476
938 Greece to 323
939 Other parts of ancient world

940 History of Europe

940 History of Europe
941 British Isles
942 England & Wales
943 Germany & neighboring central European countries
944 France & Monaco
945 Italy, San Marino, Vatican City, Malta
946 Spain, Andorra, Gibraltar, Portugal
947 Russia & neighboring east European countries
948 Scandinavia
949 Other parts of Europe

950 History of Asia

950 History of Asia
951 China & adjacent areas
952 Japan
953 Arabian Peninsula & adjacent areas
954 India & neighboring south Asian countries;
955 Iran
956 Middle East (Near East)
957 Siberia (Asiatic Russia)
958 Central Asia
959 Southeast Asia

960 History of Africa

960 History of Africa
961 Tunisia & Libya
962 Egypt, Sudan, South Sudan
963 Ethiopia & Eritrea
964 Morocco, Ceuta, Melilla Western Sahara, Canary Islands
965 Algeria
966 West Africa & offshore islands
967 Central Africa & offshore islands
968 Republic of South Africa & neighboring southern African countries
969 South Indian Ocean islands

970 History of North America

970 History of North America
971 Canada
972 Mexico, Central America, West Indies, Bermuda
973 United States
974 Northeastern United States (New England & Middle Atlantic states)
975 Southeastern United States (South Atlantic states)
976 South central United States
977 North central United States
978 Western United States
979 Great Basin & Pacific Slope region of United States

980 History of South America

980 History of South America
981 Brazil
982 Argentina
983 Chile
984 Bolivia
985 Peru

986 Colombia & Ecuador

987 Venezuela

988 Guiana

989 Paraguay & Uruguay

990 History of other areas

990 History of Australasia, Pacific Ocean islands, Atlantic Ocean islands, Arctic islands, Antarctica, extraterrestrial worlds

991-992 *Not assigned or no longer used*

993 New Zealand

994 Australia

995 New Guinea & neighboring countries of Melanesia

996 Polynesia & other Pacific Ocean islands

997 Atlantic Ocean islands

998 Arctic islands & Antarctica

999 Extraterrestrial worlds

6

Library Management

MANAGEMENT THEORIES AND THEIR PRO-FOUNDERS

Sr. No	*Theory*	*Inventor*
1	Scientific Management	F.W.Taylor
2	Principles of Management	Henry Fayol
3	Management by Objectives	Peter Drucker
4	Hierarchy of Need Theory	A. Maslow
5	Theory X and Theory Y	D. McGregor
6	Motivation Hygien approach	F. Herzberg
7	Social Relation of Management	Elton Mayo

FOURTEEN PRINCIPALS OF HENRY FAYOL

Sr. No	*Theory*
1	Division of Work
2	Authority and Responsibility
3	Discipline
4	Unity of Command
5	Unity of Command

6	Subordination of Individual Interest
7	Remuneration
8	The Degree of Centralization
9	Scalar Chain
10	Scalar Chain
11	Equity
12	Stability of Tenure of Personnel
13	Initiative
14	sprit de Corps

1. Which one is the most important problem being faced by Institutional Repositories for archiving the documents?
   (A) Availability (B) Rarity
   (C) Copyright issues (D) Author's resistance
2. Who is the Father of Library Movement in USA?
   (A) F. W. Lancaster (B) Paul Wasserman
   (C) Melvil Dewey (D) Allen Kent
3. Who coined the term POSDCORB?
   (A) Henri Fayol (B) Max Weber
   (C) Gulick and Urwick (D) Wilson and Tauber
4. __________ Budgeting does not take into account what happened in the past but emphasizes on current activities.
   (A) Formula (B) Performance
   (C) Programme (D) Zero – Based
5. 'Union List' is the record of
   (A) Library members living in a Union Territory
   (B) Periodicals available in a group of libraries
   (C) Library unions located in a Union Territory
   (D) List of members of a Library Union
6. The term 'bibliometrics' was first used by

(A) S. R. Ranganathan (B) Alan Pritchard
(C) Allen Kent (D) A. C. Foskett

7. 'Half-life' in Information Science relates to
(A) Rate of obsolescence (B) Rate of growth
(C) Degree of scatter (D) Information explosion

8. The concept of Scientific Management was introduced by
(A) Henry Fayol (B) C.I. Barnard
(C) Peter Druck (D) F.W. Taylor

9. The information of MIS comes from the
(A) Internal source
(B) External source
(C) Both internal and external source
(D) None of the above

10. The back bone of any organization is
(A) information (B) employee
(C) management (D) capital

11. AI is the short form of
(A) Artificial information
(B) Artificial intelligence
(C) Artificial integration
(D) None of the above

12. The advantage(s) of transistors are
(A) They Are portable (B) Are more reliable
(C) Consume less power (D) All of the above

13. The flow of information through MIS is
(A) need dependent
(B) organization dependent
(C) information dependent
(D) management dependent

14. The elements of control will consist of

(A) Authority, Direction, Management
(B) Authority, Direction, Information
(C) Authority, Application, Management
(D) Authority, Application, Information

15. Internal information for MIS may come from any one of the following department.
(A) Customers care department
(B) HR department
(C) Marketing department
(D) Production department

16. Audit gives details about ________ to Account Payable System
(A) Account balance (B) Transaction
(C) Expenditure (D) All of the above

17. One byte is made of
(A) Four bits (B) Eight bits
(C) Twelve bits (D) Sixteen bits

18. MIS normally found in a manufacturing organization will not be suitable in the ______.
(A) Service sector (B) Banking sector
(C) Agriculture sector (D) All of the above

19. details are given by Management to Marketing Service System.
(A) Customer (B) Employee
(C) Supplier (D) None of the above

20. The basic component(s) of DSS is (are)
(A) Database (B) Model base
(C) DSS software system (D) All of the above

21. GDSS is the short form of
(A) Group Decision Support System
(B) Group Discussion Support System
(C) Group Decision Service System
(D) Group Discussion Support Source

22. Decision trees could be represented in different ways such as
    (A) Bottom to top (B) Left to right
    (C) Top to bottom (D) All of the above
23. The types of data transmission modes are
    (A) Half duplex. , Duplex. , Singlex
    (B) Half duplex. , Duplex. , Simplex
    (C) Half duplex. , Duplex. , Half Singlex
    (D) Singlex, duplex, half triplex
24. An increase in the level of 'specificity' of indexing languages results in increase in
    (A) Recall
    (B) Precision
    (C) Noise
    (D) both recall and precision
25. The term 'Exponential growth' refers to
    (A) Linear growth
    (B) Normal mode of distribution
    (C) Geometric Progression
    (D) Arithmetic Progression
26. All Union Institute for Scientific and Technical Information (VINITI) was established in
    (A) 1952 (B) 1953
    (C) 1954 (D) 1956
27. Arrange the following according to the year of establishments:
    (i) NICNET (ii) INDONET
    (iii) INFLIBNET (iv) MALIBNET
    Codes :
    (A) (iv), (i), (iii), (ii) (B) (iv), (ii), (i), (iii)
    (C) (ii), (i), (iv), (iii) (D) (i), (iii), (iv), (ii)
28. Identify the correct order as per year of establishment

(i) ASLIB (ii) IATLIS

(iii) SLA (iv) ALA

Codes :

(A) (iv), (iii), (i), (ii) (B) (iv), (ii), (i), (iii)

(C) (ii), (i), (iv), (iii) (D) (i), (ii), (iii), (iv)

29. Match the following :

List – I	List – II
(a) SENDOC	(i) Social Sciences
(b) INPADOC	(ii) Sciences
(c) NASSDOC	(iii) Patents
(d) INSDOC (NISCAIR)	(iv) Small Scale Industries

Code :	(a)	(b)	(c)	(d)
(A)	(ii)	(iii)	(iv)	(i)
(B)	(i)	(ii)	(iii)	(iv)
(C)	(iv)	(iii)	(i)	(ii)
(D)	(iii)	(iv)	(i)	(ii)

30. Match the following

List – I	List – II
(a) Best books for the largest numbers	(i) D.B. Krishna Rao
(b) Library is the heart of all university work	(ii) B.S. Kesavan
(c) First Ph.D. in Library Science	(iii) S. Radhakrishnan
(d) First Librarian of National Library (India)	(iv) Melvil Dewey

Code :	(a)	(b)	(c)	(d)
(A)	(i)	(ii)	(iii)	(iv)
(B)	(iv)	(iii)	(ii)	(i)
(C)	(iii)	(iv)	(i)	(ii)
(D)	(iv)	(iii)	(i)	(ii)

31. Which type of books should be weeded in a library?
    (A) Superseded editions (B) Thesaurus
    (C) Dictionary (D) Encyclopaedia
32. According to General Financial Rules, 2005, loss of how many volumes per thousand volumes issued / consulted in a year is to be taken as reasonable.
    (A) Three (B) Four
    (C) Five (D) Six
33. According to Ranganathan, many collections lose its relevance in how many years?
    (A) 20 years. (B) 30 years
    (C) 40 Years (D) 50 years.
34. Annual withdrawals from the collection should average at least how many percent of the total collection.
    (A) 5% (B) 10%
    (C) 15% (D) 20%
35. The word Archives is most relevant to
    (A) Historical material (B) National bibliography
    (C) Free of charge (D) Family members
36. The word Referral service is most relevant to
    (A) Database search service
    (B) Inter Library Loan
    (C) Information scouting
    (D) Retrospective searching
37. Dr. S. R. Ranganathan related to
    (A) The disciple of Melvil Dewey who worked in India
    (B) The first professionally qualified university librarian in India
    (C) He for the first time in India, DDC and AACR rule introduced.
    (D) The first librarian of the Imperial Library

38. First university to introduce MPhil and PhD in LIS in India
    (A) Aligarh Muslim University
    (B) University of Calcutta
    (C) University of Delhi
    (D) University of Madras
39. UGC Curriculum Development Committee formed in
    (A) 1993 (B) 1991
    (C) 1968 (D) 1989
40. CCF was developed by
    (A) UNESCO (B) IFLA
    (C) FID (D) Library of Congress
41. The UNESCO Public Library Manifesto was last revised in
    (A) 1956 (B) 1931
    (C) 1972 (D) 1994
42. Peter A. Phyer related to
    (A) Ranganathan formulated his first law of library from his casual hint.
    (B) Library legislation
    (C) Living with book
    (D) Zero Based Budget
43. The First and Oldest University Library was established in British India at
    (A) University of Delhi
    (B) Calcutta University
    (C) Aligarh Muslim University
    (D) University of Madras
44. George Kingsely Zipf related to
    (A) Psycho-biology of language An introduction to dynamic philosophy
    (B) Mathematical Theory of Information
    (C) Information is data of value to decision making
    (D) Bradfords Law of Information

45. WIPO was established by the WIPO Convention in
    (A) 1977 (B) 1944
    (C) 1954 (D) 1967
46. E. B. Ross related to
    (A) Ranganathan formulated his first law of library from his casual hint
    (B) Library legislation
    (C) Living with book
    (D) Zero Based Budget
47. The Head Office of IASLIC located at
    (A) Kolkata (B) Delhi
    (C) Mumbai (D) Chennai
48. Michael Gorman related to
    (A) Application of Ranganathan's Laws to the Web
    (B) The disciple of Melvil Dewey who worked in India
    (C) Our Singular Strengths
    (D) The first librarian of the Imperial Library (now National Library, Kolkata)
49. M. C. Yovits related to
    (A) Psycho-biology of language An introduction to dynamic philosophy
    (B) Information is data of value to decision making
    (C) Mathematical Theory of Information
    (D) Bradfords Law of Information
50. First B.Lib. Science Course was introduced in
    (A) Aligarh Muslim University
    (B) University of Calcutta
    (C) University of Delhi
    (D) University of Madras
51. UNIMARC was developed by
    (A) UNESCO (B) IFLA
    (C) FID (D) Library of Congress

52. Universal Copyright conventions was in
(A) 1949 (B) 1952
(C) 1971 (D) 1931

53. Haines related to
(A) Ranganathan formulated his first law of library from his casual hint.
(B) Library legislation
(C) Living with book
(D) Zero Based Budget

54. Melvin J. Voigt
(A) Categorized information need into current approach, everyday approach, and exhaustive approach.
(B) Divides documentary sources of information into primary and secondary.
(C) Divides documentary sources of information into primary, secondary and tertiary.
(D) Classified documentary sources of information into Conventional, Neo Conventional, Non Conventional and meta document.

55. GSDL was developed at
(A) Massachusetts Institute of Technology (MIT) libraries & Hewlett-Packard labs
(B) Katipo Communications Ltd, New Zealand
(C) University of Waikato, New Zealand.
(D) Wikimedia Foundation

56. The first university to establish a full-fledged Department of Library Science
(A) University of Delhi
(B) Calcutta University
(C) Aligarh Muslim University
(D) University of Madras

57. Berne convention was adopted in the year
    (A) 1911 (B) 1886
    (C) 1900 (D) 1947
58. FID was dissolved in the year
    (A) 2002 (B) 2005
    (C) 2000 (D) 2003
59. PERT was developed by
    (A) The Navy special project office
    (B) Booz Allen Hamelton
    (C) Both (A) and (B)
    (D) None of the above
60. Million Book Project was initiated by
    (A) Pittsburg University
    (B) Carnegie Mellon University
    (C) MIT, USA
    (D) Michigan University
61. The quotation Where is the Wisdom, We Lost in Knowledge...... is by
    (A) John Keats (B) M. P. Carter
    (C) T. S. Eliot (D) Marshall McLuhan
62. CONPOLIS (India) was set up in the year
    (A) 1985 (B) 1986
    (C) 1987 (D) 1988
63. First time efforts for the development of libraries in India were made
    (A) S. R. Ranganathan
    (B) S. Radhakrishnan
    (C) Sayaji Rao Gaekwad I
    (D) Sayaji Rao Gaekwad III
64. The UNESCO Public Library Manifesto first issued in
    (A) 1949 (B) 1952
    (C) 1971 (D) 1931

65. Who is the propounder of the term information transfer?
    (A) Ranganathan (B) J. Martin
    (C) Beesman (D) Calvin Moores
66. When Peter F. Drucker defined M.B.O. (Management by Objectives)?
    (A) 1950 (B) 1960
    (C) 1954 (D) 1964
67. Who said the demand and supply theory of books?
    (A) Melvil Dewey (B) Dr. S. R. Ranganathan
    (C) Mc Colvin (D) Sayers
68. "To provide the best books to the maximum readers at the least cost" said by
    (A) Dr.S.R. Ranganathan (B) P. N. Kaula
    (C) E.Mayo (D) Melvil Dewey
69. Theory X and Theory Y is developed by
    (A) Louis Brandeis (B) Douglas Mc Gregor
    (C) Abraham Maslo (D) Mayo
70. Herzberg's theory deals with
    (A) Staffing (B) Directing
    (C) Motivation (D) Planning
71. Who is the father of Scientific Management
    (A) F.W. Taylor (B) Harold Koontz
    (C) Peter F. Drucker (D) Luther Gulick
72. CPM (Critical Path Method) is developed by
    (A) Dupoint Company (B) Aircraft Corporation
    (C) IIM (D) IBM
73. Main use of Shelf list is
    (A) Cataloging (B) Circulation
    (C) Stock Verification (D) Book Selection
74. Zero Base Budgeting system was propounded by
    (A) Peter F. Drucker (B) P.N. Kaula
    (C) E.Mayo (D) Peter Phyr

75. What are methods copying based on Silver halide processes

1. photostat
2. microfilm
3. electrography
4. Mimeography

(A) 1,2 (B) 3,4
(C) 1,2,3 (D) 1,2,3,4

76. When Zero Base Budgeting system was first prepared

(A) 1950 (B) 1960
(C) 1970 (D) 1980

77. TQM is a system of continuous improvement employing participative management and centered on needs of the ________

(A) Customers (B) Staff
(C) Organization (D) Government

78. Financial support given to libraries are of two types - Recurring and

(A) Ad-hoc (B) Endowments
(C) Annual (D) Non-recurring

79. Principle of maximum aggregate benefit is concerned with__

(A) Growth of library (B) Library use
(C) Library service (D) Library fee

80. .... takes items of expenditure for libraries as the working data for allocation of funds.

(A) Method of details (B) Per capita method
(C) Principle of economy (D) Library budget

81. A budget which mainly covers items of current revenue and expenditure is called

(A) Programme budget (B) Welfare economics
(C) Current budgeting (D) Capital budgeting

82. The library budget of a university is passed by the?

(A) Senate (B) Executive Council
(C) Academic Council (D) Research Council

83. The current newspapers are displayed on
    (A) Reading table (B) Pending racks
    (C) Pigeon Holes (D) Stacks
84. In fund accounting, _______ fund can not be used for other purposes.
    (A) Recurring (B) Non-recurring
    (C) Restricted (D) Encumbering
85. Scrutiny of financial transactions is called
    (A) Budgeting (B) Programming
    (C) Accounting (D) Auditing
86. What are the two parts of the annual report of the library
    (A) Primary and Secondary
    (B) Analytical and Systematic
    (C) Upper and Lower
    (D) Descriptive and Statistical
87. Who is the pioneer of open access system in British libraries
    (A) Nine e.Brown (B) James Duff Brown
    (C) John cotton dana (D) S. R. Ranganathan
88. Who started New York Charging system?
    (A) Peter Drucker (B) Elton Mayo
    (C) John Cotton Dana (D) Francis Bacon
89. When did electrically operated book charging system introduced first?
    (A) 1926 (B) 1905
    (C) 1933 (D) 1932
90. How many columns are there in the accession register?
    (A) 10 (B) 12
    (C) 14 (D) 16
91. When was PERT developed?
    (A) 1958 (B) 1968
    (C) 1955 (D) 1948

92. Who had invented the MBO?
    (A) Eltomn Mayo
    (B) Frederic Winslow Taylor
    (C) Peter Drucker
    (D) Kermeth Blanchard
93. PPBS relates to
    (A) Book selection (B) Journal selection
    (C) Budgeting (D) Library records
94. The standard "X" and theory "Y" was conceived by
    (A) Peter F.Drucker (B) Doughlas Mc Gregor
    (C) Gulik and Urwick (D) Taylor
95. Duplicate microfilm Rolls are preserved at
    (A) Below 27 degree C temperature
    (B) Room temperature
    (C) Anywhere in the room
    (D) Air conditioned room with normal temperature
96. Who is the father of Classical School
    (A) Lyndall Urwick (B) Gulick
    (C) Cutter (D) Henri Fayol
97. Another term of PERT is
    (A) CPM (B) POSDCORB
    (C) MBO (D) HRM
98. Short title usually found tooled on the spine of the book is
    (A) Alternative Title (B) Fanciful Title
    (C) Binder's Title (D) Tell-Tale Title
99. what are the standard size of the Accession Register is
    (A) 16" * 12" (B) 16" * 13"
    (C) 16" * 11" (D) 16" * 18"
100. A good library building is an outcome of librarian and.
    (A) Registrar (B) Building Corporation
    (C) Finance Officer (D) Architect

101. The marketing concepts in Library Service include
   (A) analysis, planning, implementation and control
   (B) advertising, planning, analysis and control
   (C) distribution, control, analysis, implementation
   (D) indexing, planning, control and implementation.

102. There are a few basic factors which may be applied in winning the hearts of the readers. They are
   (A) Psychological factor, environmental factor, social factor
   (B) Self factor, psychological factor, service factor
   (C) Service factor, philosophical factor, self factor
   (D) Technological factor, service factor, self factor

103. Is an important record of books, which shows the position of any book on the shelves.
   (A) Bay Guide (B) Authority File
   (C) Accession List. (D) Shelf list

104. Books lost from the library are known through
   (A) Stock verification
   (B) Charging and discharging
   (C) Shelf list
   (D) Accession Register

105. The first centre to use computer in the library and information activities in India is
   (A) DESIDOC (B) INSDOC
   (C) DRTC (D) UGC

106. Special libraries get their funds from
   (A) Library tax (B) Cess
   (C) Library fee (D) Their parental body

107. Staffing is concerned with providing and maintaining .... resources.
   (A) Physical (B) Technical
   (C) Human (D) Financial

108. Which of the following is not a document

(A) Book
(B) Periodical
(C) Inscription
(D) Machine Readable Catalogue

109. Which of the following guides are used in maintenance section in library

(i) Gangway guides (ii) Shelf guides
(iii) Tier guides (iv) User guides

Codes:

(A) (i), (ii) and (iv) are correct
(B) (i), (ii) and (iii) are correct
(C) (ii), (iii) and (iv) are correct
(D) (i), (iii) and (iv) are correct

110. Library Ethics is combination of what?

(i) Responsibility (ii) Accountability
(iii) Commitment (iv) Decision Making

Codes:

(A) (i), (ii) and (iii) are correct
(B) (ii), (iii) and (iv) are correct
(C) (ii), (iii) and (iv) are correct
(D) (i), (ii) and (iv) are correct

111. Which of the following guides are "TQM" tools

(i) Fishbone Diagram (ii) Histogram
(iii) Pie Chart (iv) Run Charts

Codes:

(A) (i), (iii) and (iv) are correct
(B) (i), (ii) and (iv) are correct
(C) (ii), (iii) and (iv) are correct
(D) (i), (ii) and (iv) are correct

112. Intellectual property means?

(A) Books (B) All reading material
(C) Intellectual thoughts (D) All of the above

113. Most commonly used script in the world is:

(A) Cyrillic (B) Tibetan

(C) Hebrew (D) Roman

114. Who suggested the Seven Lamps of Conducts as must for library professional

(A) Joint council of Library Association in India (JOCLAI)

(B) Indian Library Association

(C) S.R.Rangnathan

(D) R. L . Mittal

115. The Principal which states that if the facet B in a subject will not be operative without the Concept behind A is conceded then B should follow A is known as:

(A) Wall Picture Principal

(B) Principal of Parsimony

(C) Principal of Osmosis

(D) Law of Impartiality

116. which of the following display racks are used to display print periodical publication

(i) Kardex (ii) Step type

(iii) Pigeon hole type (iv) Inclined type

Codes :

(A) (i), (ii) and (iii) are correct

(B) (ii), (iii) and (iv) are correct

(C) (i), (iii) and (iv) are correct

(D) (i), (ii) and (iv) are correct

117. Name of the Indian Librarian Who was honored with the title of "Khan Bahadur" in 1935 by the British Government

(A) S. R. Rangnathan (B) B. S. Kesavan

(C) K. M. Asadullah (D) K. Isaac

118. The record associated with genealogy file might reasonably be arranged in a

(A) Clustered file (B) Tree-Structured File

(C) Hashed Files (D) Indexed Files

119. Mathch the following

(A) Nominal Scale i. Temperature measurement

(B) Ordinal Scale ii. Gender as variable

(C) Interval Scale iii. Ranking of Library Services

(D) Ratio Scale iv. Mass of a body

Codes:

(A) iii, iv, ii, i (B) ii, iii, iv, i

(C) ii, iii, i, iv (D) i,iv,iii.ii

120. Which one is not a Canon (as given by Ranganthan)?

(A) Canon of Comprehensiveness

(B) Canon of Consistence

(C) Canon of Context

(D) Canon of Currency

121. Physical condition of the books should be property maintained This is known as

(A) Collation. (B) Conservation

(C) Shelf-arrangement (D) Organization

122. Match the following:

(1) Scientific Management (a) Peter Drucker

(2) Theory of Motivation (b) Maslow

(3) Theory of X and Y (c) F. W. Taylor

(4) MBO (d) McGregor

Codes :

(A) c, b, d, a (B) b, a, c, d

(C) d, b, a, c (D) a, d, c, b

123. Bench marking, SWOT analysis and Environmental Scanning activities should occur continually and consistently in Library's strategic planning process to ensure that

(A) the organisation is competitive and enabled to meet future needs as they occur.

(B) not to modify or update mission statements of the organisation periodically.

(C) to keep the library stakeholders under cloud about the forward movement of the organisation.

(D) to derecognise the faster movement of technology.

124. **Assertion (A) :** Maximum use of library resources is the motto of the library.

Reason (R) : It satisfies the fifth law of library science.

(A) Both (A) and (R) are true.

(B) Both (A) and (R) are false.

(C) (A) is true, but (R) is false.

(D) (A) is false, but (R) is true.

125. **Assertion (A) :** Authority work deals with formulation and recording of authorized access points.

Reason (R) : Without authority control, the burden is placed on user.

(A) Both (A) and (R) are true.

(B) Both (A) and (R) are false.

(C) (A) is true, but (R) is false.

(D) (A) is false, but (R) is true.

126. **Assertion (A) :** Total quality in organization usually depends upon the skill and competency of library staff.

Reason (R) : Quality management is an information-based management system where professional education alone helps the employee to take decisions judiciously.

(A) (A) is false, but (R) is true.

(B) Both (A) and (R) are true.

(C) (A) is true, but (R) is false.

(D) Both (A) and (R) are false.

ANSWERS

1 (C)	2 (C)	3 (C)	4 (B)	5 (B)	6 (B)
7 (A)	8 (D)	9 (C)	10 (A)	11 (B)	12 (D)
13 (A)	14 (A)	15 (A)	16 (A)	17 (B)	18 (A)
19 (C)	20 (D)	21 (A)	22 (D)	23 (B)	24 (B)
25 (C)	26 (A)	27 (D)	28 (A)	29 (C)	30 (D)
31 (A)	32 (C)	33 (A)	34 (A)	35 (A)	36 (C)
37 (B)	38 (C)	39 (A)	40 (A)	41 (D)	42 (D)
43 (B)	44 (A)	45 (D)	46 (A)	47 (A)	48 (C)
49 (B)	50 (A)	51 (B)	52 (B)	53 (C)	54 (A)
55 (C)	56 (A)	57 (B)	58 (A)	59 (A)	60 (B)
61 (C)	62 (A)	63 (D)	64 (A)	65 (C)	66 (C)
67 (C)	68 (D)	69 (B)	70 (C)	71 (A)	72 (A)
73 (C)	74 (D)	75 (A)	76 (C)	77 (C)	78 (B)
79 (C)	80 (D)	81 (D)	82 (B)	83 (A)	84 (A)
85 (D)	86 (D)	87 (B)	88 (C)	89 (D)	90 (C)
91 (A)	92 (C)	93 (C)	94 (B)	95 (A)	96 (D)
97 (A)	98 (C)	99 (B)	100 (D)	101 (B)	102 (D)
103 (D)	104 (B)	105 (B)	106 (D)	107 (C)	108 (C)
109 (B)	110 (A)	111 (D)	112 (D)	113 (D)	114 (A)
115 (A)	116 (B)	117 (C)	118 (B)	119 (A)	120 (A)
121 (B)	122 (A)	123 (A)	124 (C)	125 (A)	126 (C)

7

Computer and ICT

1. Binary System of numbers uses only
   (A) Two Digits (B) Four Digits
   (C) Eight Digits (D) Six Digits
2. Xerographic process is categorized under
   (A) Photographic Process
   (B) Reflex Method
   (C) Silver halide Process
   (D) Electrostatic Process
3. RSS feed is a tool of ....
   (A) Graphic design
   (B) Web 1.0
   (C) Web 2.0
   (D) Architecture which of the following cannot be regarded as 'multimedia'
4. which of the following cannot be regarded as 'multimedia'
   (A) A tape-slide programme
   (B) A CD-ROM with text and visuals
   (C) Microfilm
   (D) A web page

5. One of the following search engine is exclusively meant for scientific information:
   (A) Google (B) Yahoo
   (C) SCIRUS (D) Altavista
6. GIF Stands for:
   (A) Graphics Interchange Format
   (B) Graphics Internet Format
   (C) Graphics Interchange File
   (D) Graphics Internet File
7. What is a database?
   (A) Printed information sources
   (B) Non paper information sources
   (C) Non printed information sources
   (D) Electronic forms of printed source
8. Which of the following languages is more suited to a structured program?
   (A) FORTRAN (B) BASIC
   (C) PASCAL (D) None of the above
9. A computer assisted method for the recording and analyzing of existing or hypothetical systems is
   (A) Data transmission (B) Data flow
   (C) Data capture (D) Data processing
10. The brain of any computer system is
    (A) ALU (B) Memory
    (C) CPU (D) Control unit
11. What difference does the 5th generation computer have from other generation computers?
    (A) Technological advancement
    (B) Scientific code
    (C) Object Oriented Programming
    (D) All of the above

12. Which of the following computer language is used for artificial intelligence?
    (A) FORTRAN (B) PROLOG
    (C) C (D) COBOL
13. Which of the following is the 1's complement of 10?
    (A) 01 (B) 110
    (C) 11 (D) 10
14. Which part interprets program instructions and initiate control operations.
    (A) Input (B) Storage unit
    (C) Logic unit (D) Control unit
15. Any type of storage that is used for holding information between steps in its processing is
    (A) CPU (B) Primary storage
    (C) Intermediate storage (D) Internal storage
16. are software which is used to do particular task.
    (A) Operating system (B) Program
    (C) Data (D) Software
17. How many generations of computers we have?
    (A) 6 (B) 7
    (C) 5 (D) 4
18. The difference between people with access to computers and the Internet and those without this access is known as the:
    (A) digital divide. (B) Internet divide.
    (C) cyberway divide. (D) Web divide
19. The term 'Pentium' is related to
    (A) DVD (B) Hard Disk
    (C) Microprocessor (D) Mouse
20. Feedback mechanism is a part of which service?
    (A) Reprography service (B) CAS
    (C) Translation service (D) SDI

21. What is a collection of terms or records in MARC called?
    (A) System (B) Network
    (C) Website (D) Database

22. The improvement of computer hardware theory is summarized by which law.?
    (A) Metcalf's law (B) Bill's Law
    (C) Moore's First Law (D) Grove's law

23. Which of the following are open source content management systems?
    (A) Drupal (B) Atex
    (C) Joomla (D) OpenCms

    Codes :
    (A) (i), (iii) and (iv) are correct
    (B) (i), (ii) and (iii) are correct
    (C) (ii), (iii) and (iv) are correct
    (D) (iii), (i) and (iv) are correct

24. A computer that connects one network to another for the purpose of file transfer is known as ...
    (A) Highway (B) Search Engine
    (C) Gateway (D) Super way

25. Microchip was invented by ...
    (A) Microsoft (B) IBM
    (C) DELL (D) Intel

26. Which is the first compiler-level language developed by a team of IBM programmers led by John Backus and unveiled in 1957?
    (A) BASIC (B) PL/1
    (C) FORTRAN (D) APL

27. Reinterpretation is a digital preservation strategy where curator intends to
    (A) Upgrade file format
    (B) Upgrade storage mechanism

(C) Recreate a work

(D) Upgrade Operating System

28. Which of the following is not correctly matched?

(A) DELNET - Library Network

(B) Digital Library - Print Material

(C) Thesaurus - List of Descriptors

(D) ISSN - Serial Number

29. Technological Gatekeeper is:

(i) An informal channel

(ii) A term coined by T.J. Allen

(iii) A formal channel

(iv) A term coined by Derek De J. Solla Price

Codes :

(A) (i) and (ii) are correct

(B) (i) and (iii) are correct

(C) (ii) and (iii) are correct

(D) (iii) and (iv) are correct

30. In which of the following network topologies, all the computers are connected to a central computer?

(A) Ring (B) Star

(C) Bus (D) Peer to Peer

31. Formatting a document in Computer means:

(A) Editing the content

(B) Changing the appearance

(C) Adding new content

(D) Changing the font size only

32. Which of the following search devices will lead to an increase in the Recall output ?

(A) Boolean 'And' (B) Boolean 'Not'

(C) Proximity Operators (D) Truncation

33. **Assertion (A) :** Computerization of Public Libraries in India is slow.

Reason (R) : Non-availability of resources.

(A) (A) is true but (R) is false
(B) (R) is true but (A) is false
(C) Both (A) and (R) are true
(D) Both (A) and (R) are false

34. A number of devices that are related to recall and precision have been studied by
(A) Gilchrist (B) Vickery
(C) Lancaster (D) Ranganathan

35. MARC was started in the year
(A) 1962 (B) 1975
(C) 1966 (D) 1985

36. ....is a process of Information
(A) Books (B) CD-ROM
(C) Computers (D) None of the above

37. Which terms was coined by S.R. Ranganathan for mobile libraries
(A) Moving library (B) Library on wheels
(C) Library machine (D) All of the above

38. **Assertion (A) :** Systems analysis identifies the flow of work.

Reason (R) : Systems analysis is not necessary if the library is to be automated.
(A) Both (A) and (R) are correct
(B) Both (A) and (R) are false
(C) (A) is true and (R) is false
(D) (R) is true and (A) is false

39. the chronological sequence of the technology is
(A) Telephone, Television, Satellite Communication, INTERNET
(B) Telephone, Satellite Communication, Television, INTERNET
(C) Telephone, Television, INTERNET, Satellite Communication
(D) Telephone, INTERNET, Television, Satellite Communication

40. Identify the correct order of the evolution of the following storage devices :
    (A) DVD, Magnetic tape, Floppy, CD
    (B) CD, DVD, Magnetic tape, Floppy
    (C) Floppy, CD, DVD, Magnetic tape
    (D) Magnetic tape, Floppy, CD, DVD
41. Identify the correct order of evolution of computers:
    (A) PC-XT, PC-AT, Main frame, Micro
    (B) PC-AT, PC-XT, Main frame, Micro
    (C) Micro, PC-AT, PC-XT, Main frame
    (D) Main frame, Micro, PC-AT, PC-XT
42. The Physical medium through which the signal is transmitted to the receiver is known as
    (A) Source (B) Transmitted
    (C) Code (D) Optical Signal
43. **Assertion (A) :** Users can have access to large number of E-journals through consortia.
    Reason (R) : Users are not aware of using web-resources.
    (A) (A) is false and (R) is true
    (B) (A) is true and (R) is false
    (C) Both (A) and (R) are true, but (R) is not the right explanation of (A)
    (D) Both (A) and (R) are false
44. Which one of the sequences is in ascending order ?
    (A) Bytes, Gigabytes, Megabytes, Terrabytes
    (B) Bytes, Megabytes, Gigabytes, Terrabytes
    (C) Bytes, Terrabytes, Megabytes, Gigabytes
    (D) Megabytes, Bytes, Terrabytes, Gigabytes
45. Match the following :

List-I	List-II
(a) Search Engine	(i) Internet Explorer
(b) Subject Gateway	(ii) Dogpile
(c) Net Browser	(iii) FTP
(d) Meta Search Engine	(iv) SOSIG
	(v) Altavista

Code :	(a)	(b)	(c)	(d)
(A)	(iv)	(iii)	(ii)	(i)
(B)	(v)	(iv)	(i)	(ii)
(C)	(v)	(i)	(ii)	(iii)
(D)	(v)	(i)	(iv)	(ii)

46. Identify the correct order of evolution of the following storage order.
    (A) Paper, Micro card, Magnetic tape, Clay tablet
    (B) Clay tablet, Paper, Micro card, Magnetic tape
    (C) Micro card, Magnetic tape, Clay tablet, Paper
    (D) Magnetic tape, Clay tablet, Paper, Micro card
47. GUI stands for :
    (A) Graphic User Interface
    (B) Graphic User Interaction
    (C) Graphic Utility Interface
    (D) Great Union of India
48. Who enunciated the term 'hypertext'?
    (A) E. Garfield (B) Bill Gates
    (C) Ted Nelson (D) Raj Reddy
49. COPSAT stands for
    (A) Cooperative periodicals in science and technology
    (B) Current online periodicals in science and technology
    (C) Current online patent in science and technology
    (D) Contents of periodicals in science and technology
50. Tagging in web 2.0 application is called :
    (A) Taxonomy (B) Folksonomy
    (C) Syndication (D) Directory
51. Norbert weiner regarded as the father and developer of the field of
    (A) Informatics (B) Bibliometrics
    (C) Cybermetrics (D) Econometrics

52. Mozilla is
    (A) An operating system (B) Library software
    (C) A web browser (D) A search engine

53. High Level Language is
    (A) Disk space dependent
    (B) O. S. dependent
    (C) Machine independent
    (D) Machine dependent

54. Protocol means
    (A) Interchange of data between two devices
    (B) Interchange of data between two computers
    (C) Linkage between two computers
    (D) Linkage between two devices

55. A set of rules that govern overall data communications system is populurly known as..
    (A) Protocol (B) Agreement
    (C) Pact (D) Memorandum

56. Which of the following is not true about e journals?
    (A) They are distributed through digital methods
    (B) They also have editors or editorial boards
    (C) They are publications of serial nature
    (D) They are always free of cost

57. Which are the facets relating to INFLIBNET?
    (a) CALIBER (b) PLANNER
    (c) UGC-INFONET (d) SOUL
    Of these :
    (A) (a), (c) and (d) (C) (a). (b) and (c)
    (B) (c), (b) and (a) (D) all of these.

58. CD-ROM is an example of
    (A) Optical Media (B) Magnetic Media
    (C) Hyper Media (D) A.V.Media

59. What is not open source software for library management?
(A) KOHA (B) AVANT1
(C) php my Library (D) 2.39-50.

60. which one of the following protocols is used in transferring file over internet?
(A) POP (B) FTP
(C) SMTP (D) TCP/IP

61. Transistors were used in which generation of computers?
(A) First generation (B) Second generation
(C) Third generation (D) None of the above

62. Linux is an example of
(A) Application software (B) System software
(C) Library software (D) All of the above

63. Ventura, Page make are example of
(A) Hardware (B) Software
(C) Operating System (D) Server

64. How different nodes in a network are connected and how they communicate are determined?
(A) By Network Connectivity
(B) By Network Topology
(C) By Network Compatibility
(D) None of the above

65. **Assertion (A) :** Electronic access to information is becoming easy day by day.
Reason (R) : The printed materials pouring out of the world presses do not show any decline.
(A) Both (A) and (R) are true but (R) is not a correct explanation of (A).
(B) (A) is true but (R) is false.
(C) (A) is false but (R) is true.
(D) Both (A) and (R) are false.

66. **Assertion (A) :** Use of microfilming is becoming obsolete day by day.

Reason (R) : ICT has developed digital technologies, which are quick, cheap and easy to handle.

(A) Both (A) and (R) are true but (R) is not a correct explanation.

(B) Both (A) and (R) are false.

(C) (A) is true but (R) is false.

(D) Both (A) and (R) are true and (R) is the correct explanation of (A).

67. **Assertion (A):** Libraries are changing in the wake of emerging ICT environment.

Reason (R) : Libraries are adopting new competencies to operate services in the environment of information super highways.

(A) Both (A) and (R) are true.

(B) (A) is true but (R) is false.

(C) (A) is false but (R) is true.

(D) Both (A) and (R) are false.

68. Arrange the following in chronological sequence:

(I) Digital Millennium Copyright Act

(II) Right to Information Act. (India)

(III) Information Technology Act (India)

(IV) Indian Copyright Act

Codes :

(A) (IV), (I), (III), (II) (B) (IV), (II), (III), (I)

(C) (I), (IV), (II), (III) (D) (II), (III), (I), (IV)

69. Arrange the following software's according to their development :

(I) E-Print (II) D-space

(III) Greenstone (IV) Koha

Codes :

(A) (IV), (III), (II), (I) (B) (III), (II), (I), (IV)

(C) (I), (II), (III), (IV) (D) (II), (III), (IV), (I)

70. Arrange the following chronologically according to their development:

(I) Punched Card (II) Floppy Disc

(III) Magnetic Disc (IV) Optical Disc

Codes :

(A) (II), (III), (I), (IV) (B) (I), (III), (II), (IV)

(C) (I), (II), (III), (IV) (D) (IV), (I), (II), (III)

Read the following passage and mark your answers for questions from (71 to (75):

In economics, inflation refers to a rise in the general level of prices of goods and services over a period of time. It reflects erosion in the purchasing power of money. When the general price level rises, the purchasing power of money comes down as each unit of currency buys fewer goods and services. Originally the term inflation was used to refer to the amount of money in circulation. The principal measure of inflation is the inflation rate, the annualized percentage change in Consumer Price Index over time. Inflation impacts an economy in various ways; it can have simultaneously both positive and negative effects. The negative effects include: a decrease in the real value of money and other monetary items over time; As there is uncertainty over future inflation, it may discourage investments and savings; and high inflation may lead to shortages of goods if consumers begin hoarding out of concern that prices will increase in the future. The huge increase in the retail prices of onions, vegetables and other commodities in India is an example of the effect of inflation. It also has positive effects; e.g. a high rate of inflation encourages investment in non-monetary capital projects. A high rate of inflation is generally the result of excessive growth in money supply. However, several different factors including growth in money supply may cause low to moderate rates of inflation. The factors could include fluctuations in the demand for goods and services, or changes in available supplies (as during scarcities). In any case most economists concede that a long and sustained period of inflation is the result of money supply growing faster than the rate of "economic growth. Most economists favor a low (as opposed to zero or negative) steady rate of inflation as a low rate of inflation may reduce the severity of economic recessions by enabling the labor market to adjust more quickly in a downturn, and reduce the risk that a liquidity trap prevents monetary policy from stabilizing the economy. In any country the responsibility of keeping the rate of inflation low and stable is that of the central bank as this is the agency that controls the volume of money supply by setting interest rates, through open market operations, and through the setting of banking reserve requirements. Inflation is certainly not a new phenomenon. It has occurred throughout history. For example, when gold was the currency, governments would mix lesser metals such as silver, lead or copper with gold to make coins. While these coins retained their nominal value, the diluting of gold with lesser metals allowed governments to issue more coins without increasing the amount of gold required to make these coins thus increasing money supply; but the practice also resulted in lowering the relative value of the money. The wide adoption of paper currency by countries in the 18th Century resulted in even larger variations in money supply. Measuring inflation in a country requires an objective means of differentiating changes in nominal prices of a common representative set of commodities and services. For this a price index, which represents the combined price of a large basket of representative goods and services is used. Inflation measures are also modified over time. Historically a good of literature that studies inflation exists. The primary focus has been on identifying factors that lead to inflation. There are two broad theories that seek to explain inflation: the Quality Theory and the Quantity Theory. There is also a relation between inflation and employment. A certain level of inflation is considered desirable in order to minimize unemployment.

71. The relation between inflation and employment is:
    (A) There is no relation between inflation and employment
    (B) Inflation leads to unemployment
    (C) Inflation leads to under-employment
    (D) Inflation helps reduce unemployment
72. The factor that is believed to cause inflation is
    (A) The switch to paper currency from gold currency
    (B) The fall in the production of goods
    (C) The increase in money supply
    (D) An increase in the general level of prices of commodities
73. Inflation in a country is measured based on
    (A) The consumer price index
    (B) The volume of money supply
    (C) The exchange rate of currency
    (D) The quantum of reserve gold available in the country
74. For the proper growth of an economy, economists generally favour
    (A) A negative rate of inflation
    (B) A high rate of inflation
    (C) A zero rate of inflation
    (D) A low rate of inflation
75. In India the agency responsible for monitoring the rate of inflation is

(A) Reserve Bank of India
(B) Ministry of Finance, Government of India
(C) The State Bank of India and its subsidiaries
(D) The Ministry of Trade & Commerce, Government of India

76. World Wide Web was first designed by
(A) Charles Babbage (B) F.W. Lancaster
(C) Ted Nelson (D) Tim Berner's Lee

77. Dublin core meta data consists of
(A) 15 elements (B) 10 elements
(C) 25 elements (D) 08 elements

78. Use of integrated circuits was made in
(A) First Generation Computers
(B) Second Generation Computers
(C) Third Generation Computer
(D) Fourth Generation Computers

79. The Network Topology in which nodes are connected to a central hub is known as
(A) Ring Topology (B) Bus Topology
(C) Star Topology (D) Mesh Topology

80. The Input Centre for INIS in India is
(A) DRDO (B) DSIR
(C) TFIR (D) BARC

81. DELNET stands for
(A) Developing Library Network
(B) Department of Electronics Library Network
(C) Distance Education Library Network
(D) Delhi Library Network

82. **Assertion (A) :** Data base is a collection of interrelated data stored together.

Reason (R) : It is an organised, integrated collection of data.

Codes :

(A) Both (A) and (R) are false.

(B) (A) is false, but (R) is true.

(C) Both (A) and (R) are true.

(D) (A) is true, but (R) is false.

83. Information Technological year was adopted in

(A) 1980 (B) 1982

(C) 1983 (D) 1984

84. which two organizations jointly publish survey on digitization and preservation?

(A) IFLA + UNESCO (B) ALA + UNESCO

(C) IFLA + ALA (D) IFLA + LC

85. which is the focus of system emulation

(A) Developing systems that mimic hardware

(B) Developing systems that mimic software

(C) Developing systems that file formats

(D) none of the above

86. which of the following is a multi-subject gateway?

(A) Renardus (B) Humbul

(C) Sapling (D) EdWEb

87. Which of the following is a specialized information organization online tool?

(A) Mamma (B) Dogpile

(C) Vivisimo (D) Entireweb

88. What is the meaning of E-Documents?

(A) All Documents other than printed

(B) Non-Paper documents

(C) In electronic form such as Cassettes, CD-ROMs, etc.

(D) Audio visual tools

89. Internet Public Library is being maintained by?
(A) MIT, Massachusettes
(B) University of Michigan
(C) Oxford University
(D) Drexal University

90. Shodhgangotri is a repository of?
(A) E-Books (B) E Journals
(C) E Thesis (D) E Synospsis

91. Relational Database is
(A) A work which has some relationship to another work
(B) A symbol representing relationship between two concepts
(C) Manipulation commands which relate records in different fields
(D) all of the above

92. The Complete bibliographic details in MARC are available in
(A) Leader (B) Control fields
(C) Variable fields (D) Record Directing

93. JSTOR is an online system for archiving and accessioning academic journals, It is located in
(A) Germany (B) UK
(C) USA (D) Budapest

94. The term "Cyberspace" was first used by
(A) Andrew Pollock (B) William Gibson
(C) John Postal (D) Joe Flower

95. The term hypertext was coined by whom?
(A) Ted Nelson (B) Vannevan Bush
(C) John Brown (D) J. C. Kith

96. Dublin core metadata consists of
(A) 13 elements (B) 10 elements
(C) 11 elements (D) 12 elements

97. Annual Convention of INFLIBNET organized by discuss the progress of the library automation and library services is known as?
    (A) ISCON (B) NACLIN
    (C) CALIBER (D) INFONET
98. Which helps to creation of an in house digital library?
    (A) LIBSYS (B) Greenstone
    (C) Alice or windows (D) Micro CDS/ISIS
99. NICNET and INDONET are the networks of which category?
    (A) LAN (B) MAN
    (C) WAN (D) CAN
100. NACLINE is sponsored by
    (A) INFLIBNET (B) DELNET
    (C) AGRINET (D) CALIBNET
101. conversion of barcode into electrical signals by
    (A) Scanners (B) CRT
    (C) Photo sensors (D) UNICODE
102. Which is not a programming language?
    (A) FORTON (B) BASIC
    (C) COBOL (D) ASCII
103. OCLC is
    (i) Online Computer Library Centre
    (ii) At Dublin (Ohio)
    (iii) At New York
    (iv) Ohio College Library

    Codes :
    (A) (i) and (ii) are correct
    (B) (i) and (iii) are correct
    (C) (iii) and (iv) are correct
    (D) (ii) and (iv) are correct

104. ENIAC stands for?
    (A) Electronic Numerical Integrator and Calculator
    (B) Electrified Numerical Integration and Calculator
    (C) Electronic Number Integrator and Calculator
    (D) Electrical Numerical Integrator and Calculator
105. ISO-9960 is related with?
    (A) Standard for encoding data on CD-ROM
    (B) Standard for Computer Hardware
    (C) Standard for Information Processing
    (D) Standard for Networking
106. ASCII has how many codes?
    (A) 256 (B) 526
    (C) 265 (D) 254
107. Raw, unevaluated, unprocessed and unorganized facts is known as:
    (A) Data (B) Information
    (C) Knowledge (D) Wisdom
108. INTERNET was initially developed by US Department of
    (A) Commerce (B) Defense
    (C) Interior (D) State
109. Information retrieval is fastest from
    (A) Floppy Disk (B) Magnetic Tape
    (C) Hard Disk (D) None of the above
110. An University providing Open Access to Sanskrit dissertations through Internet
    (A) Jawaharlal Nehru University
    (B) Delhi University
    (C) Mahatma Gandhi University
    (D) University of Madras
111. in which of the following the term "Truncation" is used
    (A) Budgeting (B) Search Formulation
    (C) Coordination (D) Classified bibliography

112. The term "Hypertext" was coined by
   (A) Garfield (B) Bill Gates
   (C) Ted Nelson (D) Raj Reddy
113. UNIX is a
   (A) Single user operating system
   (B) Double user operating system
   (C) Triple user operating system
   (D) Multi user operating system
114. ISDN stands for
   (A) Integrated Services Digital Network
   (B) Information Server for Digital Network
   (C) Integrated Server for Digital Network
   (D) Information Service For Data Network
115. LYCOS is a
   (A) search engine (B) programming language
   (C) database (D) database vendor
116. why digital objects become in accessible quickly?
   (A) Because of unforeseen advancement of technology
   (B) it is independent of human intervention
   (C) it is independent of any technological advancement
   (D) None of the above
117. Following is not a social bookmarking site:
   (A) Digg (B) Delicious
   (C) Sqidoo (D) Facebook
118. Following is not a network protocol:
   (A) HTTP (B) SMTP
   (C) TCP/IP (D) **Z39.50**
119. LOCKOSS (Software) is an international community initiative by:
   (A) MIT Libraries
   (B) Stanford University
   (C) University of Waikato
   (D) University of Southampton

120. Identify the odd one from the following:
(A) Koha (B) VTLS
(C) SLIM++ (D) SOUL

121. Following is not a Web 2.0 tool:
(A) Blog (B) Facebook
(C) UGC-INFONET 2.0 (D) RSS feeds

122. PDA stands for:
(A) Personal Digital Assistance
(B) Personal Document Archive
(C) Personal Digital Archive
(D) Program Download Accessories

123. PLONE is a:
(A) Content Mnagement System
(B) Digital Library Software
(C) ILMS
(D) Federated Search Engine

124. Following is an example of microblogging:
(A) Wordpress (B) Blogspot
(C) Livejournal (D) Twitter

125. Who invented OSI Model in 1982
(A) BSO
(B) ISI
(C) Indian standerd orgganisation
(D) International standard organisation

126. Where ISDN was first started in 1990
(A) USA (B) UK
(C) India (D) Singapore

127. Now-a-days how many types of Protocol are used ?
(A) 5 (B) 4
(C) 3 (D) 2

128. which type of protocol is used by interface for public data network (PDN)?

(A) X.25 (B) X.12
(C) X.13 (D) X.20

129. CCF stands for
   (A) Common Communication Format
   (B) Centre for Communication Format
   (C) Committee for Communication Format
   (D) Common Curriculum Format

130. In Which five year plan the INFLIBNET was established
   (A) Fourth five year plan
   (B) Fifth five year plan
   (C) sixth five year plan
   (D) seventh five year plan

131. INFLIBNET headquarters is located at
   (A) Gandhinagar (B) New Delhi
   (C) Bangalore (D) Chennai

132. Resource sharing is a part of
   (A) Library cooperation (B) Library administration
   (C) Library management (D) Library cataloguing

133. What is the full form of ERNET
   (A) Engineering Network
   (B) Eastern Regional Network
   (C) Electronic Research Network
   (D) Education and Research Network

134. which network in India provided the first e-mail service in the country?
   (A) NICNET (B) DELNET
   (C) ERNET (D) INFLIBNET

135. what is full text e-Resource?
   (A) JCCC (B) ISID
   (C) Science finder scholar(D) ACS

136. Virtual accommodates Different version of the MARC Standard?

(A) USMARC
(B) UKMARC
(C) CANMARC
(D) SWEMARC/All of above

137. The Electronic Library is
(A) A Magazine (B) A Journal Name
(C) A Library (D) An Encyclopedia

138. what is e-prints?
(A) A catalogue
(B) A journal
(C) A repository Software
(D) An encyclopedia

139. what two is a Library Management Software for small libraries?
(A) Library Solution and Follet
(B) Follet and MSN
(C) MSN and Tar
(D) LYCOS and Live Search

140. The factors that influence computer file organization are?
(A) Speed of access? (B) Storage Space?
(C) Fixed length fields (D) File Volatility.
Codes:
(A) (i), (ii), and (iii) are correct
(B) (i), (ii), and (iv) are correct
(C) (ii), (iii), and (iv) are correct
(D) (i), (ii), and (iv) are correct

141. What is APS ?
(A) A Search Engine?
(B) A Full-text e-resource
(C) Bibliographic database
(D) Library Management Software

142. "Shodhganga" is a national level repository of:
   (A) E-Books (B) E-Journals
   (C) E-Theses (D) Journal Articles
143. One of the following is not an open source software :
   (A) D'space (B) Windows
   (C) Green-stone (D) Linux
144. what are the major driving forces behind an "Information Society"
   (i) RTI (ii) ICT
   (iii) INTERNET (iv) IT Act
   Codes:
   (A) (ii) and (i) are correct
   (B) (ii) and (iii) are correct
   (C) (ii) and (iv) are correct
   (D) (iii) and (iv) are correct
145. The component of an ISO-2709 meant primarily machine processing of the record is
   (A) the Label (B) the Directory
   (C) the Datafields (D) the Record Seperator
146. which one of the following is not a part of the MARC record structure?
   (A) Leader (B) Directory
   (C) Record terminator (D) Check digit
147. Among the different Boolean operators "AND" is used
   (A) to widen the search (B) to narrow the search
   (C) to begin the search (D) to end the search
148. Windows NT is the name of
   (A) Cable TV
   (B) Network
   (C) A Computer Operating Sytem
   (D) An On-line database

149. Arrange the following chronologically according to their use in computers :

(i) Vacuum tube (iii) Integrated circuits

(ii) Microchip (iv) Transistors

Codes :

(A) (i), (iii), (ii), (iv) (B) (i), (ii), (iii), (iv)

(C) (i), (iv), (iii), (ii) (D) (ii), (iv), (iii), (i)

150. Which of the following types of memory is volatile

(A) ROM (B) PROM

(C) WORM (D) RAM

151. which of the following is not a programming language

(A) FORTRAN (B) BASIC

(C) COBOL (D) ASCII

152. when you create a worksheet in CDS/ISIS you are defining

(A) . the external user view

(B) the internal file structure

(C) he conceptual frame

(D) All of the above

153. OPAC stands for

(A) Online Public Access Catalogue

(B) Online Periodicals Access Centre

(C) Online Patents Access Centre

(D) None of the above

154. what is Dublin Core?

(A) Content management tool

(B) E- Library software

(C) Metadata standard

(D) Internet Protocol

155. Resources of Hybrid library is

(A) Print Collection (B) Digital Collection

(C) Both (A) and (B) (D) None of the above

156. who invented World Wide Web (WWW)
    (A) Vint Cerf (B) Charles Babbage
    (C) Tim Berners-Lee (D) Steve Jobs
157. Which of the following is a Library Management Software?
    (A) LibSys 7 (B) EPrints
    (C) Joomla (D) Drupal
158. Which of the following is an Open Source Software?
    (A) E-Granthalaya (B) SOUL 2.0
    (C) Koha (D) LibSys 7
159. First generation computer uses
    (A) Microprocessor
    (B) Transistors
    (C) Integrated circuits
    (D) Thermionic valves or vacuum tube or electronic valves
160. Second generation computer uses
    (A) Thermionic valves or vacuum tube or electronic valves
    (B) Microprocessor
    (C) Integrated circuits
    (D) Transistors
161. Which of the following is a social network?
    (A) BUBL Link (B) LIS Links
    (C) Intute (D) DMOZ
162. which is not a part of inflibnet
    (A) e-Vidwan
    (B) e-Acharya
    (C) Annals of Library and Information Studies
    (D) CUCOLIS
163. Koha was developed at

(A) Katipo Communications Ltd, New Zealand
(B) University of Waikato, New Zealand.
(C) Massachusetts Institute of Technology (MIT) libraries & Hewlett-Packard labs
(D) Wikimedia Foundation

164. Deleted email can be found in the
(A) Trash folder (B) Inbox folder
(C) Starred folder (D) Spam folder

165. Which of the following is an Institutional Repository Software Package?
(A) Joomla (B) EPrints
(C) Koha (D) Drupal

166. Third generation computer uses
(A) Microprocessor
(B) Transistors
(C) Integrated circuits
(D) Thermionic valves or vacuum tube or electronic valves

167. Fourth generation computer uses
(A) Microprocessor
(B) Thermionic valves or vacuum tube or electronic valves
(C) Transistors
(D) Integrated circuits

168. which of the following is not a web browser?
(A) Firefox (B) Internet Explorer
(C) Google Chrome (D) DMOZ

169. which of the following is not a Learning Management System (LMS)
(A) Moodle (B) Claroline
(C) Drupal (D) ATutor

170. DSpace was developed at

(A) Katipo Communications Ltd, New Zealand
(B) University of Waikato, New Zealand.
(C) Massachusetts Institute of Technology (MIT) libraries & Hewlett-Packard labs
(D) Wikimedia Foundation

171. The simple Dublin Core Metadata Element Set (DCMES) consists of
(A) 10 elements (B) 15 elements
(C) 14 elements (D) 18 elements

172. On which of the following technologies semantic web is not based?
(A) RDF (B) Ontologies
(C) Cloud seeding (D) URI

173. World Wide Web (WWW) was first designed by whom?
(A) Charles Babbage (B) F. W. Lancaster
(C) Ted Nelson (D) Tim Berners Lee

174. which generation computers uses integrated circuits (ICs)?
(A) First (B) Second
(C) Third (D) Fourth

175. The concept of Artificial Intelligence (AI) belongs to
(A) Second Generation Computers
(B) Third Generation Computers
(C) Fourth Generation Computers
(D) Fifth Generation Computers

176. Computer memory is measured in
(A) Bytes (B) Kilobytes
(C) Megabytes (D) All of the above

177. what are three types of basic languages used in computer programming?
(A) Zero, low and high levels
(B) COBOL, BASIC and PROLOG

(C) FOTRAN, PL/I and SNOWBOL
(D) Machine, Assembly and high level languages

178. When CD-ROM was prepared and made?
(A) 1985 (B) 1982
(C) 1980 (D) 1977

179. In how many ways switching system can be established?
(A) Two (B) Three
(C) Five (D) Seven

180. Which type of switching system is telephone network?
(A) Circuit switching (B) Packet switching
(C) Message switching (D) None of the above

181. Which of the following software is useful for word processing?
(A) DBASE (B) LIBSYS
(C) WordStar (D) CDS/ISIS

182. Who designed analytical engine?
(A) Charles Babbage (B) Pascal
(C) James watt (D) Boyl

183. Calculating machine is developed by
(A) Charles Babbage (B) Pascal
(C) Shakuntala Devi (D) Boyl

184. What is a bug?
(A) Computer Virus
(B) Error in Computer Configuration
(C) Error in a Programme
(D) None of these

185. which is not a operating system?
(A) Winzip (B) Linux
(C) Apple (D) Windows

186. Which is not word editor
(A) MSoffice (B) Notepad
(C) Openoffice (D) SQL

187. Which of the following library network?
    (A) Internet (B) Intranet
    (C) OCLC (D) Calibnet
188. Arrange the following online system according to their death of origin
    (i) ERIC (ii) MEDLINE
    (iii) OCLC (iv) MARC
    Codes:
    (A) (iv), (i), (ii), (iii) (B) (i), (iii), (iv), (ii)
    (C) (iii), (ii), (i), (iv) (D) (i), (iv), (iii), (ii)
189. Arrange the following library automation software according to their death of origin
    (i) SOUL (ii) KOHA
    (iii) New GENLIB (iv) LIBSYS
    Codes:
    (A) (iv), (i), (ii), (iii) (B) (i), (iii), (iv), (ii)
    (C) (iii), (ii), (i), (iv) (D) (iv), (i), (iii), (ii)
190. RDA Stands for
    (A) Resource Description Agency
    (B) Reference Description and Access
    (C) Reference Description Agency
    (D) Resource Description and Access
191. Which of the following is a public domain database?
    (A) INIS (B) AGRIS
    (C) Chemical Abstracts (D) MEDLINE
192. OAI Stands for
    (A) Open Access Initiative
    (B) Open Archives Initiative
    (C) On-line Archives Initiative
    (D) On-line Access Initiative
193. The 12 rules for relational database were given by
    (A) Larvy Page (B) Linus Tolward
    (C) J. Bill Gates (D) Edgar. F. Codd

194. the CD alphabets in CDS/ISIS stands for
   (A) Computerized Documentation
   (B) Condensed Disk
   (C) Confirmed Disc
   (D) Compact Disc
195. Electronic telecommunications system joining millions of computers together.
   (A) E-mail (B) Internet
   (C) US Mail (D) UPS
196. NALANDA the digital library is an initiation of
   (A) DRTC (B) IISC Banglore
   (C) NIT Calicut (D) NISCAIR
197. In Binary Numbering System digit 11 is represented by
   (A) 1010 (B) 00001011
   (C) 11011 (D) 00010110
198. Six Sigma in Quality management was developed by
   (A) Motorola (B) IIB
   (C) Honey well (D) genpact
199. What is the purpose of coockies
   (A) Identify users on the server
   (B) Act as buffer store
   (C) connect database
   (D) Develop dynamic webpages
200. PDf stands for
   (A) Pure Data Format
   (B) Portable Data Format
   (C) Portable Document Format
   (D) Pure Document Format
201. Which of the following advantageous features of portable document format (PDF)?

(i) More Compatibility
(ii) Easy Editing
(iii) Supports image format
(iv) Good Compression ration

Codes :

(A) (i) and (ii) are correct
(B) (ii) and (iii) are correct
(C) (iii) and (iv) are correct
(D) (iv) and (i) are correct

202. Arrange the following in the order their development

(A) DOS (B) MACOS
(C) Linux (D) UBUNTU

Codes:

(A) a, b, c, d (B) b, c, d, a
(C) a, c, b, d (D) b, d, a, c

203. match the following

(A) MY SQL i. Language
(B) Apache ii. Server
(C) Perl iii. User Interface
(C) API iv. RDBMS

Codes :

(A) ii, iv, iii, i (B) iv, ii, i, iii
(C) i, ii, iii, iv (D) iii, i,ii.iv

204. Match the following

(A) real time communication i. Bulletin Board
(B) Telnet ii. Subscribed membership
(C) USENET iii. Video conferencing
(D) Listserv iv. Remote login

Codes :

(A) ii, iii, iv, i (B) iii, iv, i, ii
(C) iv, ii, i, iii (D) iii,i,ii.iv

205. Blog is a?
   (A) Off-Line Journal (B) Internet Journal
   (C) Web Directory (D) Search Engine

206. **Assertion (A) :** Internet access provides information in abundance.

   Reason (R) : Information available on internet always lacks authenticity.

   Codes :

   (A) Both (A) and (R) are true and (R) is the correct explanation of (A).
   (B) (A) is false, but (R) is true.
   (C) Both (A) and (R) are true, but (R) is not a correct explanation of (A).
   (D) (A) is true but (R) is false.

207. Pi is the e-book reading device by:
   (A) Amazon (B) Sony
   (C) Infibeam (D) Nokia

208. Auto abstracting involves use of computers to
   (A) structure the content of an abstract
   (B) prepare indicative abstract
   (C) pickup significant words
   (D) arrange words in order

209. Match the following MARC21 elements with corresponding tags:

   (a) Personal Main Entry (i) 700
   (b) Personal Subject Heading (ii) 245
   (c) Personal Added Entry (iii) 100
   (d) Bibliographic Title (iv) 600

   Codes :

   (A) (i), (iv), (ii) (iii) (B) (ii), (i), (iii) (iv)
   (C) (iii), (iv), (i) (ii) (D) (iv), (ii), (iii) (i)

210. Match the following MARC21 elements with corresponding tags:

(a)	folksonomy	(i)	Tim wu
(b)	weblog	(ii)	Thomas Vander Wal
(c)	Net neutrality	(iii)	Tim Berners Lee
(d)	semantic web	(iv)	John Barger

Codes :

(A) (i), (iii), (iv) (ii) (B) (iii), (ii), (iv) (i)
(C) (ii), (iv), (i) (iii) (D) (iv), (i), (iii) (ii)

211. The main objectives of the library automation are:
(i) Monetization of library services
(ii) Establishment of a well storage and retrival system
(iii) Time and human power saving with qualitative services
(iv) Suitability for library cooperation and coordination development.

Codes :

(A) (i), (ii), (iv) (B) (ii), (iii), (iv)
(C) (i), (ii), (iii) (D) (i), (iii), (vi)

212. Which one of the following is not federated search tool
(A) MuseGlobal (B) MetaLib
(C) Webfeat (D) Yandex

213. add one out
(A) NGL (B) OPALS
(C) Evergreen (D) BiblioteQ

214. Which one is enable users to search and browse through all of library resources by replacing the traditional OPAC to include: Catalog Records, Digital Library Items, Institutional Repository, Other Library Collections and Resources
(A) Invenio (B) Koha
(C) Vufind (D) Omeka

215. Match the following MARC21 elements with corresponding tags:

(a) SLIM 21	(i) softlink
(b) Alice for windows	(ii) innovative interfaces
(c) Virtua	(iii) NIC
(d) E-granthalaya	(iv) Algorhythms

Codes :

(A) (iii), (ii), (i) (iv) (B) (iv), (i), (ii) (iii)

(C) (i), (ii), (iii) (iv) (D) (ii), (iii), (iv) (i)

216. which device of computer operation dispenses with the use of the keyboard?

(A) Joystick (B) Light pen

(C) Mouse (D) Touch

217. ASCII stands for

(A) American standard code for information interchange

(B) All purpose scientific code for information interchange

(C) American security code for information interchange

(D) American Scientific code for information interchange

218. A general purpose single-user microcomputer designed to be operated by one person at a time is

(A) Special-purpose computer

(B) KIPS

(C) M

(D) PC

219. A number that is used to control the form of another number is known as

(A) Map (B) Mask

(C) Mamtossa (D) Marker

220. Which computer has been designed to be as compact as possible?
   (A) Mini (B) Super computer
   (C) Micro computer (D) Mainframe
221. which method is used to connect a remote computer?
   (A) Device (B) Dialup
   (C) Diagnostic (D) Logic circuit
222. how many bit code is used by Murray code for TELEPRINTER machines.
   (A) 4 (B) 5
   (C) 9 (D) 25
223. The symbols used in an assembly language are
   (A) Codes (B) Mnemonics
   (C) Assembler (D) All of the above
224. A computer program that converts assembly language to machine language is
   (A) Compiler (B) Interpreter
   (C) Assembler (D) Comparator
225. The time required for the fetching and execution of one simple machine instruction is
   (A) Delay time (B) CPU cycle
   (C) Real time (D) Seek time
226. The time for which a piece of equipment operates is called
   (A) Seek time (B) Effective time
   (C) Access time (D) Real time
227. Binary numbers need more places for counting because
   (A) They are always big numbers
   (B) Any no. of 0's can be added in front of them
   (C) Binary base is small
   (D) 0's and l's have to be properly spaced apart
228. The radian of a number system

(A) Is variable
(B) Has nothing to do with digit position value
(C) Equals the number of its distinct counting digits
(D) Is always an even number

229. Which is a basic technique, using activity networks.
(A) CPA (B) VLSI
(C) GIGO (D) MSI

230. A technique for processing jobs on a first-come, first-served basis is known as
(A) FAX (B) FIFO
(C) GIGO cable (D) Optical mark reader

231. A device mounted on a communication satellite which receives, amplifies and re-transmits signals from earth station is
(A) Track (B) Transponder
(C) Transistor (D) Terminal

ANSWERS

1 (A)	2 (B)	3 (C)	4 (A)	5 (C)	6 (A)
7 (D)	8 (D)	9 (B)	10 (C)	11 (B)	12 (B)
13 (A)	14 (D)	15 (D)	16 (B)	17 (C)	18 (A)
19 (C)	20 (D)	21 (D)	22 (C)	23 (A)	24 (C)
25 (D)	26 (C)	27 (C)	28 (B)	29 (A)	30 (B)
31 (B)	32 (A)	33 (A)	34 (C)	35 (A)	36 (B)
37 (B)	38 (C)	39 (A)	40 (D)	41 (D)	42 (D)
43 (C)	44 (B)	45 (B)	46 (B)	47 (A)	48 (C)
49 (B)	50 (B)	51 (C)	52 (C)	53 (C)	54 (B)
55 (A)	56 (D)	57 (D)	58 (A)	59 (D)	60 (D)
61 (B)	62 (B)	63 (B)	64 (C)	65 (A)	66 (D)
67 (A)	68 (A)	69 (B)	70 (C)	71 (D)	72 (C)
73 (C)	74 (B)	75 (A)	76 (D)	77 (A)	78 (C)
79 (C)	80 (D)	81 (D)	82 (C)	83 (C)	84 (A)
85 (A)	86 (A)	87 (C)	88 (C)	89 (D)	90 (D)
91 (C)	92 (C)	93 (C)	94 (B)	95 (A)	96 (B)
97 (C)	98 (B)	99 (C)	100 (B)	101 (A)	102 (D)
103 (A)	104 (A)	105 (A)	106 (A)	107 (A)	108 (B)

109 (C)	110 (B)	111 (B)	112 (C)	113 (D)	114 (A)
115 (A)	116 (A)	117 (C)	118 (D)	119 (B)	120 (A)
121 (C)	122 (A)	123 (A)	124 (D)	125 (D)	126 (A)
127 (D)	128 (A)	129 (A)	130 (D)	131 (A)	132 (A)
133 (D)	134 (B)	135 (D)	136 (D)	137 (B)	138 (C)
139 (A)	140 (B)	141 (B)	142 (C)	143 (B)	144 (B)
145 (A)	146 (C)	147 (A)	148 (C)	149 (C)	150 (D)
151 (D)	152 (D)	153 (A)	154 (C)	155 (C)	156 (C)
157 (A)	158 (C)	159 (D)	160 (D)	161 (B)	162 (A)
163 (A)	164 (A)	165 (B)	166 (C)	167 (A)	168 (D)
169 (C)	170 (C)	171 (B)	172 (C)	173 (D)	174 (C)
175 (D)	176 (D)	177 (D)	178 (A)	179 (B)	180 (A)
181 (C)	182 (A)	183 (B)	184 (C)	185 (A)	186 (D)
187 (D)	188 (C)	189 (B)	190 (D)	191 (B)	192 (B)
193 (D)	194 (A)	195 (B)	196 (C)	197 (B)	198 (A)
199 (A)	200 (C)	201 (C)	202 (A)	203 (B)	204 (B)
205 (B)	206 (D)	207 (C)	208 (A)	209 (C)	210 (C)
211 (B)	212 (D)	213 (B)	214 (C)	215 (B)	216 (C)
217 (A)	218 (D)	219 (B)	220 (C)	221 (B)	222 (B)
223 (B)	224 (C)	225 (B)	226 (B)	227 (C)	228 (C)
229 (A)	230 (B)	231 (B)			

MARC TAGS AND CODES

Sr. No	*Tags*	*Codes*
1	Title Statement	245
2	Edition Statement	250
3	Fixed Fields	006/08
4	Personnel Name	100
5	Corporate Name	110
6	Meeting Name	111
7	Uniform Name	130
8	Publisher Information	260

9	Physical Description	300
10	ISBN	020
11	Location	852
12	Varying from the title	246
13	Subject added entry	6xx
14	Personal Name	600
15	Uncontrolled Term	653
16	Corporate Name	610
17	Meeting Name	611
18	Uniform title	630
19	Chronological term	648
20	Topical term	650
21	Geographical Name	651
22	Faceted Topical term	654
23	URL	856
24	Note	5xx
25	General	500
26	Formatted Contents	504
27	Biographic	504
28	With	501
29	Citation Reference	510
30	Language	546
31	Supplements	525

COMPUTER OPERATING SYSTEMS

- Microsoft Windows 7
- Ubuntu
- Windows 8
- Windows 8.1
- Windows XP Professional
- Linux Mint
- Macintosh OSX

- Android
- Windows XP
- Windows Vista
- Fedora
- Windows 10
- Mac OS X Leopard
- Windows 98
- Google Chrome OS
- Mac OS X Lion
- Mac OS X Mountain Lion
- Windows 95
- Windows 2000
- Elementary OS

WORD PROCESSOR SOFTWARE'S AND SUPPORTIVE OS

Commercial

- Apple Pages, part of its iWork suite - Mac
- Applix Word - Linux
- Atlantis Word Processor - Windows
- Documents To Go - Android, iOS, Windows Mobile, Symbian
- Final Draft Screenplay/Teleplay word processor
- FrameMaker
- Gobe Productive Word Processor
- Han/Gul (a.k.a. HWP)
- IA Writer, for Mac, iOS
- IBM SCRIPT (markup), for IBM VM/370
- IBM SCRIPT/VS, for IBM z/VM or z/OS systems
- Ichitaro - a Japanese word processor produced by JustSystems
- InCopy
- IntelliTalk
- iStudio Publisher - Mac

- Kingsoft Writer - Windows and Linux
- Mariner Write - Mac
- Mathematica - technical and scientific word processing
- Mellel - Mac
- Microsoft Word - Windows and Mac
- Microsoft Works Word Processor
- Microsoft Write - Windows and Mac (a stripped-down version of Word)
- Nisus Writer - Mac
- Nota Bene - Windows
- Polaris Office - Android and Windows Mobile
- PolyEdit
- QuickOffice - Android, iOS, Symbian
- Scrivener
- TechWriter - RISC OS
- TextMaker
- ThinkFree Office Write

Freeware

- Atlantis Nova
- Baraha Free Indian Language Software
- Jarte
- Kingsoft Writer Personal Edition
- Madhyam
- TextMaker

Online

- Adobe Pages
- Authorea - word processor for students and researchers
- Collabora/LibreOffice
- Google Docs
- Microsoft Word Online - free online service
- ThinkFree Office Write

- WriteOnline
- XaitPorter - word processor for Enterprise, allowing both single user and team collaboration approach.
- Zoho Writer

LIBRARY MANAGER SOFTWARE'S

- SOUL 2.0
- LIBMAN
- LIBSYS
- SLIM
- Library Manager
- KOHA
- E-granthalaya
- Access-IT Library
- Adlib Library
- CR2 Librarian
- Destiny Library Manager
- Library World
- 1.6 Avanti: An Open Source Library Computing System
- 1.7 PhpMyBibli: A Free Solution for the Media Library
- 1.8 GNU Library Management System (GLIBMS)
- 1.9 phpMylibrary
- 1.10 Karuna

DIGITAL REPOSITORY SOFTWARE'S

- Dspace
- Greenstone
- Calibre
- FEDORA COMMONS
- Invenio
- Omeka
- Islandora
- OPUS

COMPUTER INPUT DEVICES

- Graphics Tablets
- Cameras
- Video Capture Hardware
- Trackballs
- Barcode reader
- Digital camera
- Gamepad
- Joystick
- Keyboard
- Microphone
- MIDI keyboard
- Mouse (pointing device)
- Scanner
- Webcam
- Touchpads
- Pen Input
- Microphone
- Electronic Whiteboard
- OMR
- OCR
- Punch card reader
- MICR (Magnetic Ink character reader)
- Magnetic Tape Drive

COMPUTER OUTPUT DEVICES

- Monitor (LED, LCD, CRT etc)
- Printers (all types)
- Plotters
- Projector
- LCD Projection Panels
- Computer Output Microfilm (COM)
- Speaker(s)

- Head Phone
- Visual Display Unit
- Film Recorder
- Microfiche

COMPUTER INPUT / OUTPUT (BOTH) DEVICES

- Modems
- Network cards
- Touch Screen
- Headsets (Headset consists of Speakers and Microphone. Speaker act Output Device and Microphone act as Input device)
- Facsimile (FAX) (It has scanner to scan the document and also have printer to Print the document)
- Audio Cards / Sound Card

8

Research Methodology

1. What is a patent?
   (A) An agreement to the Government
   (B) Document of the library
   (C) An Agreement between the inventor and the Government
   (D) An Agreement between library and Publisher
2. Canon of characteristics is part of
   (A) Verbal Plane (B) Notational Plane
   (C) Idea Plane (D) Structural Plane
3. A survey of the reading habits of Childrens in North Karnataka" is an example of
   (A) Descriptive Research
   (B) Comparative Research
   (C) Exploratory Research
   (D) Diagnostic Research
4. "Controlled Group" is a term used in.............. .
   (A) Survey research
   (B) Historical research
   (C) Experimental research
   (D) Descriptive research

5. The sum of all observations divided by the number of observations is called as
   (A) Arithmetic mean (B) Median
   (C) Mode (D) Geometric mean
6. Information Science is a discipline that investigates
   (A) the properties and behaviour of information
   (B) the forces governing the flow of information
   (C) the means for processing of information for optimal uses
   (D) all of these.
7. Population of 5000 and considers it good because
   (A) he was a good researcher
   (B) he was guided by his supervisor
   (C) the populations was homogeneous
   (D) all of these
8. Which technique is generally followed when the population is finite ?
   (A) Area sampling technique
   (B) Purposive sampling technique
   (C) Systematic sampling technique
   (D) None of the above
9. The research antagonistic to ex-post facto research is
   (A) experimental studies (B) normative researches
   (C) library researches (D) all of the above
10. The experimental study is based on the law of
   (A) single variable (B) replication
   (C) occupation (D) interest of the subject
11. 'Cranfield Project' is an example of.................... .
   (A) Experimental Research
   (B) Survey Research
   (C) Case Study
   (D) Historical Research

12. What is the collection of terms or records in MARC called?
    (A) System (B) Network
    (C) Website (D) Database
13. What is Delphi method?
    (A) It is a programming language
    (B) It is a method of research
    (C) It is a software
    (D) It is used for cost-benefit analysis.
14. Which section of the library is known as hub of the staff?
    (A) Maintenance section (B) Reference section
    (C) Circulation section (D) Technical section.
15. Herzberg's is two factor theory deals with:
    (A) Staff recruitment (B) Leadership
    (C) Decision making (D) Motivation
16. If the size of the study population is very small, the following sampling method will give better results :
    (A) Purposive (B) **Stratified**
    (C) Random (D) Census
17. **Assertion (A)** : Historical, Descriptive and Experimental Methods are scientific methods.
    Reason (R) : A scientific method is one that adopts a logical and systematic procedure.
    (A) (A) is true but (R) is false
    (B) Both (A) and (R) are true
    (C) (A) is false but (R) is true
    (D) Both (A) and (R) are true, but (R) is not the correct explanation

18. Match the following:

	List-I (Research Methods)		List-II (Type)
(a)	Content Analysis	(i)	Data Collection Tool
(b)	Questionnaire	(ii)	Qualitative Methods of Analysis
(c)	Observation	(iii)	Methods of Research
(d)	Case Study	(iv)	Direct Method

Code :	**(a)**	**(b)**	**(c)**	**(d)**
(A)	(i)	(iv)	(iii)	(ii)
(B)	(ii)	(i)	(iv)	(iii)
(C)	(iii)	(ii)	(i)	(iv)
(D)	(iv)	(iii)	(ii)	(i)

19. Match the following:

	List-I		List-II
(a)	Scientific Management	(i)	sprit de crops
(b)	Unity of Command	(ii)	Peter Drucker
(c)	Management by Objectives	(iii)	Factor of Planning
(d)	Forecasting	(iv)	Efficiency and Waste Prevention

Code :	**(a)**	**(b)**	**(c)**	**(d)**
(A)	(iv)	(i)	(ii)	(iii)
(B)	(i)	(ii)	(iii)	(iv)
(C)	(ii)	(iii)	(i)	(iv)
(D)	(iii)	(i)	(iv)	(ii)

20. Match the following :

1.	Bradford's Law	(a)	Author's productivity
2.	Lotkas Law	(b)	Citation indexing
3.	Eugene Garfield	(c)	Word frequency
4.	Zip's Law	(d)	Law of scattering

Codes :

(A) 1 (a), 2 (b), 3 (d), 4 (c)

(B) 1 (c), 2 (d), 3 (b), 4 (a)

(C) 1 (d), 2 (b), 3 (a), 4 (c)

(D) 1 (d), 2 (a), 3 (b), 4 (c)

21. How is stochastic equation of information solved?
    (A) By statistical rules
    (B) By dynamic rules
    (C) By statistical and dynamic rules
    (D) None of these.

22. which research is conducted jointly by the researcher and the practitioner?
    (A) Action research (B) Fundamental research
    (C) Diagnostic Research (D) Social Research

23. Which Bibliometrics Law describes the frequency of publication by authors in a given field?
    (A) Lotka's Law (B) Zipf's Law
    (C) Bradford's Law (D) None of the above

24. When a source referred to once in the footnote is referred to again and between them no other reference (i.e. citation) intervenes, then the footnote uses the abbreviation
    (A) Ibid (B) Id
    (C) Op.Cit (D) None of the above

25. Basic Research is also known as
    (A) Pure research (B) Fundamental research
    (C) Theoretical research (D) All of the above

26. The process of creating values through the creation of time, place and form utilities is known as
    (A) Marketing (B) Advertising
    (C) Salesmanship (D) Pricing

27. **Assertion (A) :** A sample is the representation of a whole.

Reason (R) : The sample is subjected to observation and analysis.

(A) (A) is false but (R) is true.
(B) (A) is true but (R) is false.
(C) Both (A) and (R) are true.
(D) Both (A) and (R) are false.

28. **Assertion (A) :** Loose Assemblage is the process of linking together different classes.

Reason (R) : This mode was formerly known as subject bundle.

(A) (A) is false but (R) is true.
(B) (A) is true but (R) is false.
(C) Both (A) and (R) are true.
(D) Both (A) and (R) are false.

29. In "Spiral of Scientific Method", Zenith marks

(A) Facts (B) Empirical laws
(C) Fundamental laws (D) Deduced laws

30. A researcher divides the populations into PG, graduates and 10 + 2 students and using the random digit table he selects some of them from each. This is technically called

(A) stratified sampling
(B) stratified random sampling
(C) representative sampling
(D) none of these

31. Who said that members of the same species are not alike?

(A) Darwin (B) Herbert Spencer
(C) Best (D) Good

32. A researcher divides his population into certain groups and fixes the size of the sample from each group. It is called

(A) stratified sample (B) quota sample
(C) cluster sample (D) all of the above

33. Field study is related to
(A) real life situations
(B) experimental situations
(C) laboratory situations
(D) none of the above

34. Attributes of objects, events or things which can be measured are called
(A) qualitative measure (B) data
(C) variables (D) none of the above

35. An example of scientific knowledge is
(A) authority of the Prophet or great men
(B) social traditions and customs
(C) religious scriptures
(D) laboratory and field experiments

36. Generalized conclusion on the basis of a sample is technically known as
(A) statistical, inference of external validity of the research
(B) data analysis and interpretation
(C) parameter inference
(D) all of the above

37. A statistical measure based upon the entire population is called parameter while measure based upon a sample is known as
(A) sample parameter (B) inference
(C) statistic (D) none of these

38. The final result of a study will be more accurate if the sample drawn is
(A) taken randomly
(B) fixed by quota
(C) representative to the population
(D) Purposive

39. Which of the following is a non-probability sample ?
    (A) Quota sample
    (B) Simple random sample
    (C) Purposive sample
    (D) (a) and (c) both
40. Independent variables are not manipulated in
    (A) normative researches
    (B) ex-post facto researches
    (C) both of the above
    (D) none of the above
41. **Assertion (A) :** Like social scientists, the natural scientists can also collect data by conducting experiments, interviewing/observing people and reviewing literature.

    Reason (R) : Social scientists cannot be as objective as can be natural scientists.

    Codes :
    (A) (A) is true, but (R) is false.
    (B) (A) is false, but (R) is true.
    (C) Both (A) and (R) are true.
    (D) Both (A) and (R) are false.
42. Which research is also known as formulative studies?
    (A) Diagnostic Research
    (B) Exploratory Research
    (C) Comparative Research
    (D) Descriptive Research
43. Who expressed knowledge in a simple mathematical equation k(s) +_1 = k (s + _ s) ?
    (A) Fritz Machlup (B) B.C. Brooks
    (C) N.J. Belkin (D) C.E. Shannon
44. Which type of research is useful to study the reading habits, bibliotherapy, and user behaviour in the library.

(A) Theoretical research (B) Comparative Research
(C) Descriptive Research (D) Diagnostic Research

45. Which of the following is a term used for working assumption of a solution to a problem?
(A) Research (B) Hypothesis
(C) Bibliography (D) Thesis

46. Arrange the following steps in research in the sequence of their occurrence:
(A) Report writing (B) Research design
(C) Collection of data (D) Analysis of data
Codes :
(A) (III), (IV), (II), (I) (B) (I), (III), (IV), (II)
(C) (II), (III), (IV), (I) (D) (IV), (II), (III), (I)

47. **Assertion (A) :** Median is simply the middle value when the data have been arranged in ascending or descending order.
Reason (R) : Median refers to the middle value in a distribution. Codes
(A) Both (A) and (R) are true.
(B) (A) is true, but (R) is false.
(C) (A) is false, but (R) is true.
(D) Both (A) and (R) are false.

48. Why the man went to moon? is an example of
(A) Fundamental research
(B) Applied research
(C) Action Research
(D) All of the above

49. Which research is carried out in a series of cycles one improving upon the previous?
(A) Theoretical research (B) Action Research
(C) Historical research (D) None of the above

50. Exit polls to predict the results of general elections" is coming under

(A) Comparative Research
(B) Diagnostic Research
(C) Social Research
(D) Descriptive Research

51. Arrange the structure of the Research report in correct order:

(i) Table of contents	(ii) Appendices
(iii) Text	(iv) Title page

Codes :

(A) (iii), (i), (iv), (ii)	(B) (i), (ii), (iii), (iv)
(C) (ii), (iii), (iv), (i)	(D) (iv), (i), (iii), (ii)

52. When was PERT developed?

(A) 1958	(B) 1968
(C) 1955	(D) 1948

53. Who had invented the MBO?
(A) Eltomn Mayo
(B) Frederic Winslow Taylor
(C) Peter Drucker
(D) Kermeth Blanchard

54. PPBS relates to

(A) Book selection	(B) Journal selection
(C) Budgeting	(D) Library records

55. The standard "X" and theory "Y" was conceived by
(A) Peter F.Drucker
(B) Doughlas Mc Gregor
(C) Gulik and URwick
(D) Taylor

56. Zero based budget is concerned with

(A) Present	(B) Past
(C) Future	(D) Remote future

57. Who is the father of Classical School

(A) Lyndall Urwick (B) Gulick
(C) Cutter (D) Henri Fayol

58. Who coined the word POSDCORB
(A) Henri Foyal (B) Luther Gulick
(C) Herbert (D) Elizabeth stone

59. Another term of PERT is
(A) CPM (B) POSDCORB
(C) MBO (D) HRM

60. POSDCORB is related to
(A) Library cataloguing
(B) Library reference service
(C) Library administration
(D) Library automation

61. Study carrels are exclusive areas meant for..............
(A) students (B) public
(C) women (D) researchers

62. A skillful method of providing means mechanism and structural elements to. Streamline organizational work is known as _______
(A) Strategic planning (B) Role analysis
(C) Work culture (D) Autonomous planning

63. Posting the right person at the right place is called
(A) Recruitment (B) Coaching
(C) Deployment (D) Induction

64. TQM is a system of continuous improvement employing participative management and centered on needs of the ________
(A) Customers (B) Staff
(C) Organization (D) Government

65. ________ is a process of helping employees in an organization to acquire new skills and competence on a continuing basis

(A) Total Quality Management
(B) Management Information System
(C) Financial Resources Development
(D) Human Resources Development.

66. Which one of the following is not the purpose of historical research
(A) To reconstruct the past
(B) To understand significance of events
(C) To find answers to questions about the future
(D) To study cause - and effect relationship

67. Research conducted to solve any immediate problem of theory or practice at hand is known as
(A) Applied research (B) Pure research
(C) Theoretical research (D) Action Research

68. 'Cranfield Studies' are an example of :
(A) Survey Research
(B) Experimental Research
(C) Historical Research
(D) Case Study

69. Research is
(A) Searching again and again
(B) Finding solution to any problem
(C) Working in a scientific way to search for truth of any problem
(D) None of the above

70. Which of the following is the first step in starting the research process?
(A) Searching sources of information to locate problem.
(B) Survey of related literature
(C) Identification of problem
(D) Searching for solutions to the problem

71. A common test in research demands much priority on
(A) Reliability (B) Useability
(C) Objectivity (D) All of the above

72. Action research means
(A) A longitudinal research
(B) An applied research
(C) A research initiated to solve an immediate problem
(D) A research with socioeconomic objective

73. A reasoning where we start with certain particular statements and conclude with a universal statement is called
(A) Deductive Reasoning
(B) Inductive Reasoning
(C) Abnormal Reasoning
(D) Transcendental Reasoning

74. Research is conducted to
(A) Generate new knowledge
(B) Not to develop a theory
(C) Obtain research degree
(D) Reinterpret existing knowledge
Which of the above are correct?
(A) I, III & II (B) III, II & IV
(C) II, I & III (D) I, III & IV

75. Seeing a very big rally it was reported that JD will win the election, the conclusion was based on:
(A) random sampling (B) cluster sampling
(C) systematic samialing (D) purposive sampling

76. Which of the following variables cannot be expressed in quantitative terms?
(A) Socio-economic Status
(B) Marital Status

(C) Numerical Aptitude
(D) Professional Attitude

77. The essential qualities of a researcher are
(A) Spirit of free enquiry
(B) Reliance on observation and evidence
(C) Systematization or theorizing of knowledge
(D) All the above

78. In the process of conducting research 'Formulation of Hypothesis" is followed by
(A) Statement of Objectives
(B) Analysis of Data
(C) Selection of Research Tools
(D) Collection of Data

79. A research paper is a brief report of research work based on
(A) Primary Data only
(B) Secondary Data only
(C) Both Primary and Secondary Data
(D) None of the above

80. User studies in Social sciences was carried out by
(A) Kuhn (B) Brittain
(C) Line (D) Allen

81. In a thesaurus, under an item "Internal Migration", which of the following lines would you expect to find
(A) BT Migration
(B) NT Rural-to-Urgan Migration
(C) RT International Migration
(D) All of the above

82. The PERT approach is a device developed to
(A) Better utilize of time in a series of activities
(B) Allow studies to be made between people and machine

(C) Analyse a workflow to facilitate decision-making
(D) Establish quality control

83. The basic theory regarding human motivation is propounded by
(A) Taylor (B) Maslow
(C) Mayo (D) Likert

84. Select the less frequently used measures of central tendency:
1. Arithmetic mean 2. Median
3. Mode 4. Geometric mean
5. Harmonic mean
(A) 1, 2 (B) 2, 3
(C) 3, 4 (D) 4, 5

85. The method of budgeting, which is not concerned with what happened previously but is more concerned with the requirements of the future is known as
(A) Line Budget (B) Programme Budget
(C) Formula Budget (D) Zero Based Budget

86. In an empirical study on the impact of television viewing on violence, violence would be
(A) the dependent variable
(B) an independent variable
(C) an intervening variable
(D) not a variable at all

87. A big difference between the mean and median is an indication that
(A) there is a mistake in the calculation
(B) the calculation is correct
(C) there is a wide variation in the data
(D) None of the above

88. Which of the following research methods is useful in a study on measuring the active life of periodicals

(A) Survey (B) Citation Analysis
(C) Interview (D) Case study

89. An organizational structure is determined by
(A) span of control (B) hierarchy
(C) space and location
Codes :
(A) (a) and (b) (B) (b) and (c)
(C) (a) and (c) (D) All the factors

90. The spiral of scientific method involves the following steps in correct sequence :
(I) Zenith (II) Ascendant
(III) Nadir (IV) Descendant
Codes :
(A) (I), (III), (II), (IV) (B) (II), (III), (I), (IV)
(C) (III), (II), (I), (IV) (D) (I), (IV), (III), (II)

91. Arrange the following in a logical sequence :
(i) Formulation of a hypothesis
(ii) Data analysis
(iii) Selection of sample
(iv) Report writing
Codes :
(A) (i), (ii), (iii), (iv) (B) (iv), (ii), (i), (iii)
(C) (ii), (i), (iv), (iii) (D) (i), (iii), (ii), (iv)

92. Questionnaire is a
(A) Research method
(B) Measurement Technique
(C) Tool for data collection
(D) All the above

93. Mean, Median and Mode are
(A) Measures of deviation
(B) Ways of sampling
(C) Measures of control tendency
(D) None of the above

94. Rank X frequency=constant formula describes the essence of

(A) Impact (B) Zip's Law

(C) Fuzzy query (D) Lotka Law

95. Inductive logic proceeds from

(A) General to General (B) Particular to General

(C) General to Particular (D) Particular to Particular

96. Which of the following is not a "Graphic representation"?

(A) Pie Chart (B) Bar Chart

(C) Table (D) Histogram

97. Which one of the following represent graphically the data.

(A) Check sheets (B) Histogram

(C) Scatter diagram (D) Control Chart

98. Which is not a quantitative variable

(A) Age (B) Income

(C) Education (D) Distance

99. which is also called as 'technique of summated ratings'.

(A) Spearman's Rank (B) Likert scale

(C) Scatter Diagram (D) None of the above

100. "Tribes in India" is an example for

(A) Numerical variable (B) Ordinal variable

(C) Nominal variable (D) All of the above

101. Accession number of books" is an example for

(A) Nominal variable (B) Ordinal variable

(C) Numerical variable (D) All of the above

102. Coefficient of Variation is a

(A) Measures of Central Tendency

(B) Correlation

(C) Regression Analysis

(D) Measures of Dispersion

103. Entropy is a measure of
    (A) Degree of relevance of information
    (B) Quantity of irrelevant information
    (C) Degree of uncertainty in information
    (D) Degree of certainty in information

104. **Assertion (A) :** RDA replaces the General Material Designations (GMD).

    Reason (R) : The problem with the GMDs was inconsistent categorization.
    (A) Both (A) and (R) are true.
    (B) (A) is true, but (R) is false.
    (C) (A) is false, but (R) is true.
    (D) Both (A) and (R) are false.

105. **Assertion (A) :** Precision is the fraction of the documents retrieved that are relevant to the user's information need.

    Reason (R) : In practical situations, recall and precision are always inversely
    (A) (A) is false, but (R) is true.
    (B) (A) is true, but (R) is false.
    (C) Both (A) and (R) are true.
    (D) Both (A) and (R) are false.

106. **Assertion (A) :** Online survey tools such as Survey Monkey and Question Pro have made data collection, analysis and result extraction much easier and simpler.

    Reason (R) : Though these tools are being used widely without any doubt in recent time, but social research cannot rely always on the results from an online survey because of their inherent limitations.
    (A) Both (A) and (R) are true.
    (B) Both (A) and (R) are false.
    (C) (A) is true, but (R) is false.
    (D) (R) is true, but (A) is false.

107. **Assertion (A) :** Technical writing, style manuals and citation standards are essential in structuring the research report.

Reason (R) : The quality of research can be achieved only by standardizing the structure of a research report.

(A) (A) is true and (R) is false.
(B) (A) is false and (R) is true.
(C) Both (A) and (R) are true.
(D) Both (A) and (R) are false.

108. Arrange the following Cardinal Stage in the Cycle according to their order

1. Zenith
2. Nadir
3. Ascendent
4. Descendent

Codes:

(A) 1, 2, 3, 4
(B) 4, 1, 2, 3
(C) 2, 3, 1, 4
(D) 3, 4, 1, 2

109. which of the following laws comprises the Spiral of Scientific Method?

1. Fundamental laws
2. Deduced laws
3. Nadir facts
4. Empirical laws

Codes :

(A) 1,4
(B) 1,2,4
(C) 1,2,3,4
(D) 2,4

110. Match the following

(A) Quadrant I — (1) between ascendent and zenith
(B) Quadrant II — (2) between zenith and descendent
(C) Quadrant III — (3) between descendent and nadir
(D) Quadrant IV — (4) between nadir and ascendent

Codes:

(A) 1,2,3,4
(B) 2,3,4,1
(C) 3,4,1,2
(D) 4,1,2,3

111. Quadrant 1 corresponds to the stage in which involves

1. Observation are made of knowees with or without experimental inference and conditioning
2. Facts are found
3. Primary senses are used to either in their native state or with the aid of instruments
4. Progression towards ultimate generalisation

Codes :

(A) 2,3,4 (B) 1,3,4

(C) 1,2,3 (D) All of the above

112. Quadrant 2 corresponds to the stage in which involves
    1. Intellect is used either by itself or aided by machinery
    2. Reasoning is made with the aid of inductive logic
    3. Seizing of fundamental laws and their recording
    4. Inducted or empirical laws are formulated

    Codes :

    (A) 1,2,3 (B) 1,2,4

    (C) 1,3,4 (D) 2,3,4
113. Quadrant 3 corresponds to the stage in which involves
    1. Intuition of some intensity is used unmediated by the primary senses or the intellect
    2. The inducted or empirical laws stand boiled down to a very small number of fundamental laws
    3. Progression towards ultimate abstractness
    4. Seizing of fundamental laws and their recording

    Codes:

    (A) 1,2,3 (B) 1,2,4

    (C) 1,3,4 (D) All of the above
114. Quadrant 4 corresponds to the stage in which involves
    1. Reasoning with the aid of deductive logic including mathematical and other classes
    2. Progression towards concreteness
    3. Derivation of deducted laws and their recording

4. Deducted laws must include one and all of the inducted empirical laws

Codes:

(A) 1,2,3 (B) 2,3,4

(C) 1,3,4 (D) All of the above

115. Match the following

1. Zenith	(a) A position of dominance, controlling influence
2. Nadir	(b) Something that is going down
3. Ascendent	(c) The lowest point in an activity
4. Descendent	(d) The highest point of an activity

(A) a,b,c,d (B) b,a,d,c

(C) c,d,b,a (D) d,c,a,b

116. Which of the following things happen in re-entering the spiral

1. Observations and experiments are made to verify the validity of new deducedlaws
2. Further continuous observation and experiment lead to accumulation of new empirical facts

(A) 1 only (B) 2 only

(C) both 1 and 2 (D) Neither 1 Nor 2

117. Who is regarded the father of scientific social surveys?

(A) Darwin (B) Booth

(C) Best (D) None of these

118. All are example of qualitative variables except

(A) religion and castes (B) sex

(C) observation (D) interest of the subject

119. Logic of induction is very close to

(A) the logic of sampling

(B) the logic of observation

(C) the logic of the controlled variable

(D) none of the above

120. Survey study aims at:
   (i) knowing facts about the two existing situation
   (ii) comparing the present status with the standard norms
   (iii) criticising the existing situation
   (iv) identifying the means of improving the existing situation

   Codes:

   (A) (i) and (ii) only (B) (i), (ii), and (iii)
   (C) (i), (ii), (iii) and (iv) (D) (ii) and (iii) only

121. The historical research is different from experimental research in the process of
   (A) replication
   (B) the formulation of the hypothesis
   (C) the hypothesis testing
   (D) all of the above

122. A research problem is feasible only when
   (A) it is researchable
   (B) it is new and add something to knowledge
   (C) it has utility and relevance
   (D) all of these

123. Hypothesis cannot be stated in
   (A) null and question form terms
   (B) declarative terms
   (C) general terms
   (D) directional terms

124. The validity and reliability of a research will be at stake when
   (A) The author who is the source of information is biased, incompetent or dishonest
   (B) The incident was reported after a long period of time from that of its occurrence

(C) The researcher himself is not competent enough to draw logical conclusions
(D) All of the above

125. Which of the following is not an essential element of report writing?
(A) Research Methodology
(B) Reference
(C) Conclusion
(D) None of these

ANSWERS

1 (C)	2 (C)	3 (A)	4 (C)	5 (A)	6 (D)
7 (A)	8 (C)	9 (A)	10 (A)	11 (A)	12 (D)
13 (B)	14 (A)	15 (D)	16 (B)	17 (C)	18 (B)
19 (A)	20 (D)	21 (C)	22 (A)	23 (A)	24 (A)
25 (D)	26 (A)	27 (C)	28 (C)	29 (C)	30 (B)
31 (A)	32 (B)	33 (A)	34 (C)	35 (D)	36 (A)
37 (C)	38 (C)	39 (D)	40 (C)	41 (C)	42 (B)
43 (B)	44 (D)	45 (B)	46 (C)	47 (A)	48 (A)
49 (B)	50 (C)	51 (D)	52 (A)	53 (C)	54 (C)
55 (B)	56 (C)	57 (D)	58 (B)	59 (A)	60 (C)
61 (D)	62 (A)	63 (A)	64 (A)	65 (D)	66 (C)
67 (A)	68 (B)	69 (C)	70 (C)	71 (D)	72 (C)
73 (B)	74 (D)	75 (B)	76 (D)	77 (D)	78 (B)
79 (C)	80 (A)	81 (D)	82 (A)	83 (B)	84 (D)
85 (D)	86 (B)	87 (C)	88 (B)	89 (A)	90 (C)
91 (D)	92 (C)	93 (D)	94 (B)	95 (B)	96 (C)
97 (B)	98 (C)	99 (B)	100 (C)	101 (A)	102 (D)
103 (C)	104 (A)	105 (C)	106 (A)	107 (A)	108 (C)
109 (C)	110 (C)	111 (C)	112 (B)	113 (D)	114 (D)
115 (D)	116 (C)	117 (B)	118 (D)	119 (A)	120 (B)
121 (D)	122 (D)	123 (C)	124 (D)	125 (D)	

9

Important Meanings - Abbreviations

1. **A&I** - Abstracting and Indexing
2. **AACR2** - Anglo-American Cataloging Rules, Second Edition
3. **AALL** - American Association of Law Libraries
4. **AASL** - American Association of School Librarians
5. **ABAA** - Antiquarian Booksellers Association of America
6. **ACRL** - Association of College & Research Libraries
7. **AGRIS** – Agricultural Information System
8. **AHIP** - Academy of Health Information Professionals
9. **AICTE** - All India Council for Technical Education
10. **ALA** - American Library Association
11. **ALC** - Americans for Libraries Council
12. **ALCTS** - Association for Library Collections and Technical Services.
13. **ALISE** - Association for Library and Information Science Education
14. **ALISE** - Association for Library and Information Science Education

15. **ALOHA** - Astronomy Librarians of Hawaii Association
16. **ALP** – Advancement for Librarianship
17. **ANSI** - American National Standards Institute
18. **APA** - American Psychological Association
19. **ARL** - Association of Research Libraries
20. **ARLIS/ANZ** - Arts Libraries Society of Australia and New Zealand
21. **ARLIS/NA** - Art Libraries Society of North America
22. **ARLIS/UK & Ireland** - Arts Libraries Society of the United Kingdom and Ireland
23. **ARMA International** - Association of Records Managers and Administrators International
24. **ASCII** - American Standard Code for Information Interchange
25. **ASIS** - American Society for Information Science (and Technology)
26. **ASTED** - Association pour l'avancement des Sciences et TEchniques de la Documentation
27. **AV** - Audio-Visual
28. **BALID** - Bangladesh Association of Librarians, Information Scientists and Documentalists
29. **BCI** - Bar Council of India
30. **BFM** - Bibliographic File Maintenence
31. **BI** - Bibliographic Instruction
32. **BIBCO** - the monographic BIBliographic record COmponent of the Program for Cooperative
33. **BIP** - Books In Print
34. **BL** - British Library
35. **BLISc** - Bachelor of Library and Information Science
36. **BnF** - Bibliothèque nationale de France
37. **BONET** – Bombay Library Network
38. **BPL** - Boston Public Library

39. **CAHSL** - Connecticut Association of Health Sciences Librarians
40. **CALIBNET** – Calcutta Network
41. **CAPS** – Content, Abstract and Photocopy Service (INSDOC)
42. Cataloging
43. **CDA** - Communications Decency Act
44. **CDC** - Curriculum Development Committee
45. **CD-R** - Compact Disc-Recordable
46. **CD-ROM** - Compact Disc Read-Only Memory
47. **CD-RW** - Compact Disc ReWritable
48. **CDS** - Cataloging Distribution Service (Library of Congress)
49. **CDS/ISIS** - Computerised Documentation Services Intregated Set of Information System
50. **CEP** - Continuing Education Programme
51. **CILIP** - Chartered Institute of Library and Information Professionals
52. **CIP** - Cataloging-In-Publication
53. **CLA** - Canadian Library Association
54. **CLIR** - Council on Library & Information Resources
55. **CLISc** - Certificate Course in Library and Information Science
56. **CLS** - Certificate in Library Science
57. **CM Z1** - Descriptive Cataloging Manual Z1 ("Yellow Pages")
58. **CNI** - Coalition for Networked Information
59. **COMLA** - Common Welth Library Association
60. **CONSER** - Cooperative ONline SERials (PCC component)
61. **CPSO** - Cataloging Policy and Support Office (Library of Congress)
62. **CRG** – Classification Research Group

63. **CSIR** - Council of Scientific and Industrial Research
64. **CV** - Curriculum Vitae
65. **DDB** - die Deutsche Bibliothek (German National Library)
66. **DDC** - Dewey Decimal Classification
67. **DDS** - Document Delivery Service
68. **DEC** - Distance Education Council
69. **DELNET** – Delhi Library Network
70. **DESIDOC** - Defense Scientific Information and Documentation Center
71. **DEVSIS** – Development Science Information System
72. **DIRKS** - Design and Implementation of Record keeping Systems
73. **DLIS** - Department of Library and Information Science
74. **DLSc** - Diploma in Library Science
75. **DMCA** - Digital Millennium Copyright Act
76. **DOI** - Digital Object Identifier
77. **DRC** – Data Referral Centra
78. **DRM** - Digital Rights Management
79. **DRTC** - Documentation Research and Training Center
80. **DVD** - Digital Video Disc
81. **ENVIS** – Environment Information System
82. **ERIC** - Educational Resources Information Clearing house
83. **FDLP** - Federal Depotisitory Library Program
84. **FRBR** - Functional Requirements of Bibliographic Records
85. **GIF** - Graphics Interchange Format
86. **GIS** - Geographic Information Systems
87. **GPO** - Government Printing Office
88. **GUI** - Graphical User Interface
89. **HR** - Human Resources
90. **HTML** - HyperText Markup Language

91. **HTTP** - HyperText Transfer Protocol
92. **HTTPS** - HyperText Transfer Protocol Secure
93. **IALL** - International Association of Law Libraries
94. **IAMSLIC** - International Association of Aquatic and Marine Science Libraries and
95. **IASLIC** - Indian Association of Special Libraries and Information Centers
96. **IATLIS** - Indian Association of Teachers in Library and Information Science
97. **IB** - Information Behavior
98. **ICSSR** - Indian Council of Social Science Research
99. **ICT** - Information and Communication Technology
100. **IE** - Internet Explorer
101. **IFLA** - International Federation of Library Associations and Institutions
102. **IFLA** - International Federation of Library Associations and Institutions
103. **III** - Innovative Interfaces, Incorporated
104. **IIT** - Indian Institute of Technology
105. **ILA** - Indian Library Association
106. **ILL** - InterLibrary loan
107. **IMLS** - Institute for Museum and Library Services
108. **INFLIBNET** – Information and Library Network (UGC)
109. Information Centers
110. **INSDOC** - Indian National Scientific Documentation Center
111. **ISBD** - International Standard Bibliographic Description
112. **ISBN** - International Standard Book Number
113. **ISC** - Information for Social Change (Advocacy group : United Kingdom)
114. **ISP** - Internet Service Provider

115. **ISSN** - International Standard Serial Number
116. **IT** - Information Technology
117. **JAKE** - Jointly Administered Knowledge Environment
118. **JPEG** - Joint Photographic Experts Group
119. **JSTOR** - Journal STORage
120. **KWIC** - KeyWord In Context
121. **KWOC** - KeyWord Out of Context
122. **LAB** - Library Association of Bangladesh
123. **LAN** - Local Area Network
124. **LC** - Library of Congress
125. **LCC** - Library of Congress Classification
126. **LCCN** - Library of Congress Control Number
127. **LCRI** - Library of Congress Rule Interpretation(s)
128. **LCSH** - Library of Congress Subject Heading
129. **LCSH** - Library of Congress Subject Headings, aka "The Big Red Books"
130. **LFF** - LIbrarians For Fairnesss
131. **LIS** - Library and Information Science
132. **LIS** - Library and Information Science (common abbreviation)
133. **LISA** - Library and Information Science Abstracts
134. **LISA** - Library and Information Services in Astronomy
135. **LISBd** - Librarians and Information Scientists, Bangladesh
136. **LITA** - Library and Information Technology Association
137. **LOCKSS** - Lots of Copies Keep Stuff Safe
138. **LTTE** - Letter To The Editor
139. **MALS** - Master of Arts, Librarianship
140. **MARC** - MAchine Readable Cataloging
141. **MARC** - Machine Readable Catalogue
142. MARC 21 Machine Readable Catalogue 21 Century
143. **MCI** - Medical Council of India

144. Medical Library Association
145. **MFHD** - MARC Format for Holdings Data
146. **MIS** - Master of Information Science
147. MLA
148. **MLA** - Modern Library Association
149. **MLIS** - Master of Library and Information Science
150. **MLS** - Master of Library Science
151. Modern Language Association
152. **MSLIS** - Master of Science in Library and Information Science
153. Music Library Association
154. **NAAC** - National Assessment and Accreditation Council
155. **NACO** - the Name Authority COmponent of the PCC
156. **NAMTC** - National Association of Media & Tcchnology Centers
157. **NAR** - Name Authority Record
158. **NASIG** - North American Serials Interest Group
159. **NASSDOC** - National Social Science Documentation Center
160. **NCLIS** - National Commission on Libraries and Information Science
161. **NCTE** - National Council for Teachers Education
162. **ND** - No Date
163. **NISC** - National Information Services Corporation
164. **NISCAIR** - National Institute for Science Communication and Information Resources
165. **NISO** - National Information Standards Organization
166. **NLA** - Nevada Library Association
167. **NN/LM** - National Network of Libraries of Medicine
168. **NTIS** - National Technical Information Service
169. **NUC** - National Union Catalog
170. **NYPL** - New York Public Library

171. **OCLC** - Online Computer Library Center
172. **ODLIS** - Online Dictionary for Library and Information Science
173. **OED** - Oxford English Dictionary
174. **OP** - Out of Print
175. **OPAC** - Online Public Access Catalog
176. **OS** - Out of Stock
177. **PC** - Personal Computer
178. **PCC** - Program for Cooperative Cataloging (Library of Congress)
179. **PDF** - Portable Document Format
180. **PGDIT** - Post Graduate Diploma in Information Technology
181. **PGDLAN** - Post Graduate Diploma in Library Automation and Networking
182. **PLA** - Pakistan Library Association
183. **PLG** - Progressive Librarians Guild (Advocacy group : chiefly United States)
184. **PMOLIB** - Prime Minister's Office Library
185. **PO** - Purchase Order
186. **PPL** - Peace Palace Library
187. **RA** - Readers' Advisory
188. **RAK** - Regeln für Alphabetische Katalogisierung
189. **RDA** - Resource Description and Access
190. **RDF** - Resource Description Framework
191. Required to Intercept and Obstruct Terrorism Act
192. **RFID** - Radio Frequency IDentification
193. **RFK** - Regeln für die Formalkatalogisierung
194. **RFP** - Request For Proposal
195. **RIM** - Records and Information Management
196. **RLG** - Research Libraries Group
197. **RRRLF** - Raja Rammohun Roy Library Foundation
198. **RSS** - Multiple, depending on the version

199. **RSWK** - Regeln für den Schlagwortkatalog
200. **RUSA** - Reference and Users Services Association
201. **SAA** - Society of American Archivists
202. **SACO** - the Subject Authority COmponent of the PCC
203. **SCCTP** - Serial Cataloging Cooperative Training Program
204. **SCM** - Subject Cataloging Manual (Library of Congress)
205. **SIC code** - Standard Industrial Classification code
206. **SLA** - Special Libraries Association
207. **SMS reference** - Short Message Service reference
208. **SPARC** - Scholarly Publishing and Academic Resources Coalition
209. **SRRT** - Social Responsibilities Round Table (American Library Association)
210. **SSL** - Secure sockets layer
211. **SuDoc** - Superintendent of Documents
212. **t.p.** - Title page
213. **TOC** - Table Of Contents
214. **UDC** - Universal Decimal Classification
215. **UGC** - University Grants Commission
216. **URI** - Unifrom Resource Indicator
217. **URL** - Uniform Resource Locator
218. **USA PATRIOT Act** - Uniting and Strengthening America by Providing Appropriate Tools
219. **USB** - Universal Serial Bus
220. **VHS** - Video Home System
221. **VLOG** - Video (web-)log.
222. **VPN** - Virtual Private Network
223. **WAN** - Wide Area Network
224. **WLIC** - World Library and Information Congress
225. **WWW** - World Wide Web
226. **Z39.50** - is a Standard Communication Protocol

IMPORTANT MEANING, DATE AND YEARS

1. **Scopus :** Abstract and citation database of research literature
2. **J-Store (1995) :** Journal Storage
3. **Emeralds :** Full text Journal Publishers
4. **Science Direct :** Full-text scientific database
5. **ERIC :** Education Resources Information Center, is the world's largest digital library of education literature
6. **J-Gate (2001) :** J-Gate is an electronic gateway to global e-journal literature
7. **Project MUSE (1993) :** Online database of more than 200 journals from nonprofit publishers
8. **EBSCO :** Reference Databases
9. **Pubmed :** Citations for biomedical articles from MEDLINE
10. **IndMed :** A Bibliographic Database of Indian Biomedical Literature is an indexing of medical and other biomedical journals from India not cover in Medline
11. **INIS :** The INIS Database, contains over 3 million bibliographic records
12. **LISA :** Library and Information Science Abstracts is an international abstracting and indexing tool designed for library professionals and other information specialists
13. **Genamics JournalSeek :** Genamics JournalSeek is the largest completely categorized database of freely available journal information available on the internet. The database presently contains 95320 titles. Journal information includes the description (aims and scope), journal abbreviation, journal homepage link, subject category and ISSN.
14. **Econlit :** The American Economic Association's electronic bibliography, EconLit, indexes more than

thirty years of economics literature from around the world. Compiled and abstracted in an easily searchable format, EconLit is a comprehensive index of journal articles, books, book reviews, collective volume articles, working papers and dissertations

15. **REPEC :** Research Papers in economics. Collaborative volunteer effort to enhance the dissemination of research in economics. The database contains information on more than 585,000 items
16. **OCLC Worldcat :** A global catalog of library collections.
17. Tamil Nadu (formerly Madras) Public Libraries Act. 1948
18. Andhra Pradesh Public Libraries Act. 1960
19. Karnataka Public Library Act 1965
20. Maharashtra Public Libraries Act 1967
21. West Bengal Public Libraries Act 1979
22. Manipur Public Libraries Act 1988
23. Kerala Public Libraries Act 1989
24. Haryana Public Libraries Act 1989
25. Mizoram Public Libraries Act 1993
26. Goa Public Libraries Act 1993
27. Gujarat Public Libraries Act 2002
28. Orissa Public Library Act 2002
29. Uttaranchal Public Libraries Act, 2005.
30. Rajasthan Public Libraries Act 2006
31. Delhi Public Library 1951
32. DRTC, Bangalore 1962
33. Raja Ram Mohan Roy Library Foundation 1972
34. Connemara Public Library 1890
35. Khuda Baksha Oriental Public Library 1891
36. Bhandarkar Oriental Research Institute, Pune 1917
37. Rampur Raza Library, Uttar Pradesh 1774
38. State Lenin Library, Moscow 1862

39. National Library of India- 1835
40. Bibliothec Nationale, Pris (National Library, France) 1440
41. National Diet Library, Japan 1948
42. National Library, Germany 1912
43. Library of Congress, USA 1800
44. Library Association (UK)-1877 now Known as Chartered institute of Library and Information Professionals (From 2002) 1877 (now name changed in 2002 as CILIP)
45. American Library Association- 1876
46. Association of Special Libraries and Information Beureaux –ASLIB 1926
47. IFLA-1929 1929 UBC-1974, UAP-1976
48. Special Library Association(SLA) 1909
49. FID 1982
50. UNESCO 1945
51. India Library Association 1933
52. IASLIC 1955
53. RRRLF 1972
54. DDC by Melvil Dewey 1876
55. Expansive Classification by C.A. Cutter- 1879
56. Library of Congress Classification 1902
57. Subject Classification by J. D. Brown 1906
58. Colon Classification 1933
59. Bibliographic Classification by H. E. Bliss 1935
60. International Classification by F. Rider 1961.
61. Library of Congress Subject Headings 1898
62. Sears List of Subject Headings (SLSH) 1923
63. AACR first published 1908
64. MARC 1966
65. AACR-I 1967
66. CCF 1972

67. ISBD 1974
68. UNIMARC 1977
69. AACR-II 1978
70. Online Computer Library Centre (OCLC) 1967
71. Research Library Group (RLG)-RLIN 1974
72. Joint Academic Network (JANET)
73. Consortium of University Research Libraries (CURL) 1997
74. China Academic Library & Information System 1998
75. NICNET 1977
76. CALIBNET 1986
77. ERNET 1986
78. INFLIBNET 1988
79. DELNE 1992
80. ADINET 1993
81. MALIBNET 1993
82. MYLIBNET 1994
83. UGC INFONET 2002
84. HELINET 2003
85. Asia and Pacific Information Network (APIN)
86. Information Society program for Latin America and The Caribbean (INFOLAC) 1986
87. Global Network for Education in Journalism 1999
88. Orbicom 1994
89. UNESCO Network for Associated Library (UNAL)
90. UNISIST Programme 1971
91. CDS/ISIS 1985
92. WINISIS Distributed
93. SOUL 2000
94. GREENSTONE 1997
95. DSPACE 2002
96. KOHA 2000

97. NEWGENLIB 2007
98. EPRINTS 2000
99. Relational Indexing- J.E.L.Farradane 1950
100. Coats Subject Indexing- E.J. Coats 1963
101. PRECIS-Derek Austin 1974
102. POPSI- G. Bhattacharya 1964
103. Kaisers systematic Indexing 1911
104. UNITERM- Martimer Taube 1953
105. Science Citation Index 1974
106. Social Science Citation Index 1973
107. Arts & Humanities Citation Index 1978
108. Roget's Thesaurus 1852
109. Andhra Pradesh Library Association, 1914
110. Maharashtra Library Association, 1921
111. Bengal Library Association, 1925
112. Madras Library Association, 1928
113. Karnataka Library Association, 1929
114. Punjab Library Association, 1929
115. Samastha Kerala Pustakalaya Samiti, 1931
116. Bihar Library Association, 1936
117. Assam Library Association, 1938
118. Utkal Library Association, 1944
119. Kerala Library Association, 1945
120. Hyderabad Library Association, 1951
121. U.P.Library Association, 1951
122. Delhi Library Association, 1953
123. Gujarat library Association, 1953
124. Madhya Bharat Library Association, 1957
125. Gomantak Library Association, 1961
126. Rajasthan Library Association, 1962
127. Jammu & Kashmir Library Association, 1966
128. Tripura Library Association, 1967

129. Manipur Library Association, 1987
130. Mizoram Library Association, 1987
131. Meghalaya Library Association, 1994
132. Nagaland Library Association, 1996

10

One Line Question and Answers

1. Edition 23 of DDC was published in the year 2011.
2. You can find a reference to Library hand in Classified Catalogue Code (book written by Dr. S. R. Ranganathan).
3. Institute of Scientific Information was established by Eugene Garfield
4. Dr. S. R. Ranganathan was awarded Padma Shri in the year 1957.
5. POPSI was devised by G. Bhattacharya
6. DOI stands for Digital Object Identifier
7. ILA was formed in the year 1933
8. The sectoral centre NICDAP of NISSAT is in Lucknow
9. Bibliography of bibliographies is a Tertiary source of information.
10. eGyanKosh is associated with IGNOU (institution)
11. DRTC was established in the year 1962
12. Dr. S. R. Ranganathan's autobiography is titled as A Librarian looks back
13. One place theory is associated with J.D. Brown

14. Management is an example of Distillation (mode of formation of subject)
15. Dr. S. R. Ranganathan was honoured with the title National Research Professor in the year 1965.
16. Charles Ammi Cutter brought out Dictionary catalogue in the year 1876.
17. Dr. S. R. Ranganathan initially had a post graduate degree in Mathematics
18. OSI model has Seven layers.
19. Gandhiana is a result of Clustering (mode of formation of subject)
20. RRRLF was formed in the year 1972
21. IPO : United Nations
22. Digital watermarking is part of : Steganography
23. Information Ice berg : 1/3 Visible 2/3 Non- Visible
24. A Proxy server is used for : Share Internet Links
25. Library warrant : W.Hulme
26. Barcode system uses one of the following technologies : Pattern Recognition
27. Information observed and reported by some one else is know as : Empirical Information
28. Brain Storming : Alex Osborn
29. IV volume of 20th DDC : Relative Index
30. Data Ware house is : An Electronic Repository Of Organizational Data
31. World Intellectual property day : April 26 , 2009
32. Cyberspace is not wires cables and microwave but : A Physical Place
33. The book "S.R. Ranganathan : Pragmatic Philosophy of Information Science A Personal Biography"
34. Perochial Libraries : Thomas Bray
35. TQM needs : Concept Oriented Management
36. Acronym : Donald Davinson

37. First Public Library Act : Madras
38. Already the world is well into the third great phase of Human history - the information age
39. Articulated by : Alvin Toffler
40. Buffer overflow : An Attack By Computer Hacker
41. An equivalent of Is 14000 standards is : ISO 9000
42. In flowchat Activity is represented by : Rectangle
43. One of the following is not a cause for obsolescence of published literature : No Longer Valid
44. Gantt chat : Horizontal Bar Chat
45. M in five fundamental categories (PMEST) : Matter
46. Value added information model for evaluating information systems and centres was provided by : Robert S Taylor
47. Soul 2.0 is complaint to : Ncip2.0
48. OSI Stands for : Open System Interconnection
49. ISO standard for Dublic core Metadata elements set is : Iso 15836 : 2009
50. Seymour Lubetzky was associated with : Catalogue Codes
51. VIRUS : Vital Information Resources Under Siege
52. The largest unit of a database : A File
53. The term " Exponential Growth refers to : Geometrical Progression
54. The exhaustiveness of indexing system will : Increase Precision
55. ILA : 1933 (Indian Library Association)
56. DELNET : WAN (Wide Area Network)
57. Recommended 6.5% of university budget : Radhakrishna Committee
58. Second Generation computers is : Transistor
59. Where is wisdom we have lost in knowledge : T.S. Eliot
60. Bradford formulated the law of scatter : 1948

61. Saraswathi mahal library : Maraja Sarafoji
62. Invisible colleges : Derek De Solla Price
63. Half life of information is : Rate of Obsolescence of Information
64. First university to introduced M.Phil Programm is LIS 1980 : University of Madras
65. Not a image format : Uap
66. KWIC index was : H P Luhn
67. Graphical representation of data on y-axis is : Quadrant
68. Z39.50 : Client Server Protocol
69. Phenomena of literature on a subject appearing in periodical devoted to other subject is know as : Scatter
70. Which of five laws of library science strongly advocated adv of open access : First Law
71. BIOS : Basic Input/Output System
72. Punjab Library Primer : A D Dickinson
73. Classification : Grouping And Arrangement Of Entities
74. LIS – FORUM : NCSI
75. Starvation policy : Revision of UDC
76. Five Laws of library science : 1931
77. Documentation was brought : S C Bradford
78. Wisdom of mass principle : Wikipaedia
79. Thesaurofacet : Jean Aitchison
80. Central tendency : Average
81. Atom index : INIS
82. Free floating subdivisions : Library of Congress Subject Headings
83. Shanon and weaver theory of information is based on : Mathematical Theory
84. Bodlein library is the university library of : Oxford University
85. A patent may be granted for a new useful and non obvious : Innovation

86. Facebook is a : Social Networking Site
87. World cat is : OCLC
88. Direct method of electro static copying is : Xerography
89. Focus is a : Facet
90. Encyclopedia of library and information science is published by : Marcel Dekkav
91. CCDare : UNDP (United Nations Development Programme)
92. RSS in internet terminology means : Rich Site Summary
93. The organizational structure is determined by : Span Of Control
94. See also cross reference normally represent : Associate Relations
95. Research done to find a solution for an immediate problem is known as : Applied Research
96. The term Informatics was coined by : Otto Nache
97. Laissez – faire is : Allow To Act
98. The diffusion of innovationa and its acceptance normally follows : S-Shaped Curve
99. The periodical " college and research Libraries is published by : ALA
100. First Ph.d in the LIS in India : 1958
101. John cotton Dana : ALA
102. Indian Reference sources is : J.S.Sharma
103. Youtube is associated with : Google
104. Computer virus is a : Computer Programme
105. Lotka laws is concerned with : Productivity of Authors (Dought)
106. Library pathfinders : Referral Service
107. Charles ammi cutter : Rules For Dictionary Catalogue
108. Coden is : Sericals
109. Method of experimental enquiry was advocated by : J S Mills

110. Truncation device is used to improve : Precision (Dought)
111. Maximum storage space is available on : Hard Disk
112. Demand Theory of Books selection was coined by : L R Mccolvin
113. The Hyderabad public libraries Act was : 1960 (Actualy 1955)
114. SRELS Journals : Bangalore
115. ATM stands for : Asynchronous Transfer Mode
116. OCR is a : Input Device
117. IASLIC bulletin is a : Quarterly
118. Acheme of role operators are used in : Précis
119. Intellectual property rights are a bundle of exclusive rights over creation of the mind covering : Both Artistic And Commercial Creations
120. CODATA was establish by : ICSU
121. Which one of the following has accelerated the growth of electronic publishing : Optical Median
122. Weka is a : Data Mining Software
123. Cumulative book index is a : Trade Bibliography
124. Field tag in MARC : Directrory
125. The inverse square law is the law referred to : Lotks'S Law
126. As per internet standard terminology RFC refrs : Request For Comments
127. Manual of library economy was : Brown
128. ISBD : IFLA
129. Five new laws of library sicence have been offered n 1995 by : Crwford And Gorman
130. The papyrus one of the earliest writing materials was mainly used by : Egyptians
131. Decimal classification completed hundred years in : 1976

132. Principle of recency is releated to : Library Publicity
133. Computers process data into information by working exclusively with : Multimedia
134. Relics are sources of information for : Historical Research
135. Median is not affected by : Different Values
136. The acronym UBC coined by : Donald Davinson
137. Name given by S R Ranganathan to book mobile : Librachine
138. Information as a flow and knowledge as stock : Marshall Mchuhan
139. CCF : UNESCO
140. Which one of the following is an indological library : Adayar Public Library, Chennai
141. The idea of bibliographic coupling was first advocated by : M.M. Kessler
142. Canan for verbal plane are : Four
143. Baud rate is used to measure : The Speed of Data Transmission in Telecommunication
144. ERNET is : Education And Research Network
145. Term "epitome" : Review
146. Thomas website is associated with : Thomas Publishers And Co
147. Who coined the word ROBOT : Karl Capek
148. Notation does not make a classification but it may mare it : Wc. Berwick Sayers
149. Farmingtio plan was initiated in uK in the year : 1948
150. A postulate is a : A Self Evident Statement About The Possibility Of A Thing
151. PROLOG : Programming In Logic
152. Which of the following is not a house keeping operation in library : Reference

153. AGRIS regional centre for European countries in located at : Philippines
154. GPSS : Gateway Packet Switched Service
155. Which of the following evaluation techniques is used in forecasting : Delphi Technique
156. The earliest style of chines writing was mainly : Pictographic
157. V-mail : War Time
158. Digital library of resource of Indian cultural heritage has been named as : Kalanadhi
159. Ugc-net consist of : 4 Sections
160. First Librarian of national library of india was : B.S Kesavan
161. Indcat is a online union cataloge maintained by e : Inflibnet
162. Digital library of india is hosted by : IIS

YEAR WISE DEVELOPMENT OF LIBRARY AND INFORMATION SCIENCE

1792 Bibliothec Nationale, Paris (National Library of France)

1800 Library of Congress, the national and parliamentary library of the USA was established.

1836 Calcutta Public Library (India) was opened to the public.

1837 (14 March)– Birth of C.A. Cutter in Boston

1848 Boston Public Library Act

1850 (14 August)–First Library act at National Level in the world, United Kingtom

1851 (10 Dec)–Birth of Melvil Dewey in Adams Centre, near Water town, New York

1852 Roget's Thesaurus

1862 State Lenin Library, Moscow, Russia

1862 (6 Nov)– Birth of James Duff Brown in Edinburgh.

1870 (20 Jan)—H.E. Bliss, The creator of Bibliographic Classification was born. Considered to be one of the Greatest Classificationist produced by the USA

1876 Dewey Decimal Classification devised by Melvil Dewey

1876 Formation of American Library Association (ALA), the oldest library association in the world.

1877 (5 Oct)—Library Association (UK) was founded.

1879 Expansive Classification by C.A. Cutter

1887 Melwil Dewey founded the First School for Librarianship in the world at Columbia

1891 Imperial Library, Calcutta (India)

1892 (9 Aug)— Birth of Dr. S.R. Ranganathan in Shiyali, Tanjore District of Madras State. But in Official Records, 12th of August has came into use as his Date of Birth.

1898 Library of Congress Subject Headings

1901 Library of Congress Shared Cataloguing service

1902 Library of Congress Classification

1905 First edition of the Universal Decimal Classification was published

1906 Subject Classification by J. D. Brown

1908 Anglo American Code

1909 Special Libraries Association (SLA) was formed, Special librarians in the field of chemistry are the first professionals to specialize in chemical information science

1911 Kaisers systematic Indexing

1912 National Library of Germany

1914 (10 April)—The first Conference of the Andhra Desa Librarians was held at Bezawada (Vijayawada) which resulted in the formation of the first library association in India. i.e. The Andhra Desa Library Association.

1915 Adams Report (U.K)

1923 Sears List of Subject Headings (SLSH)

1924 Mitchell and Kenyon Report

1924 (4th Jan)—Dr.S.R. Ranganathan took charge of the Madras University Library is Librarian.

1924 Indian Library Journal was first Library Journal in English published in India

1926 Association of Special Libraries and Information Beureaux (ASLIB)

1927 International Federation of Library Associations (IFLA) was established

1931 Madras University was the first University that started full time Diploma course in Library Science in India

1933 Colon Classification by Dr. S.R. Ranganathan

1933 (13, September)—Indian Library Association (ILA) was formed at the First All India Library Conference at Calcutta.

1933 First All India Library Conference at Calcutta (India)

1935 Bibliographic Classification by H. E. Bliss

1939 (10 March)—The Delhi Library Association was formed.

1942 McColvin Report (U.K)

1946 Establishment of UNESCO.

1948 Government of India changed the name of the Imperial Library to the National Library, with the enactment of the Imperial Library (Change of Name) Act, 1948

1948 (25 Nov)—First Public Library Act (Madras, Tamil Nadu) Passed in India

1948 National Diet Library, Japan

1948 (7 March)— Dr. S.R. Ranganathan was conferred with the Honorary degree of Doctor of Letters by the Governor-General of India, Lord Mountbatten the then Chancellor of the University of Delhi.

1948 University of Delhi was first university in India that

provided the facilities for conducting Masters Degree (M.Lib. Sc.) and Ph.D

1950 Relational Indexing by J.E.L.Farradane

1950 (4 Jan) – The first issue of the British National Bibliography (BNB) was brought out.

1951 (27 Oct) – Inauguration of the Delhi Public Library (DPL) by late Pt. Jawaharlal Nehru.

1952 (24 March) – Indian National Scientific Documentation Centre (INSDOC) was set up in New Delhi by Govt. of India with the help from UNESCO

1953 The National Library of India is opened for Public

1953 UNITERM by Martimer Taube

1955 Indian Association of Special Libraries and Information Centres (IASLIC) was founded at Kolkata (India)

1955 Post-Coordinate Indexing UNITERM by Martimer Taube

1957 (29) – Padmasri was awarded to Dr. S.R. Ranganathan by the President of India, Dr. Rajendra Prasad.

1957 First International Study Conference on Classification was held at Dorking (England)

1959 Robert Report (U.K)

1961 International Classification by F. Rider

1962 (18 Aug) – DRTC, Bangalore was inaugurated by Dr. C.D. Deshmukh.

1963 Coats Subject Indexing by E.J. Coats

1964 Public Library and Museum Act

1964 UGC-UK (Parry Committee Report)

1964 POPSI by G. Bhattacharya

1965 (22 April) – The Mysore Public Libraries Act came into effect.

1966 MARC

1967 AACR-I

1967 Online Computer Library Centre (OCLC)

1971 UNISIST Program

1972 Common Communication Format (CCF)

1972 (22 May)—Establishment of Raja Rammohun Roy Library Foundation at Kolkata (India)

1972 (27 Sep)—Dr. S.R. Ranganathan breathed his last at Bangalore.

1972 INPADOC (International Patents Documentations Centre, Vienna) was founded on agreement between the Republic of Austria and WIPO

1973 (2 July)—The British Library was established in London

1973 Social Science Citation Index

1974 ISBD

1974 Universal Bibliographic Control (UBC)

1974 Science Citation Index

1974 Research Library Group (RLG)-RLIN

1974 PRECIS by Derek Austin

1976 UAP

1977 UNIMARC

1978 AACR-II

1978 Arts & Humanities Citation Index

1982 FID

1985 Library Management Software and Digital Library Software CDS/ISIS

1992 Centaury Year of Dr. S.R. Ranganathan

1993 Project Muse

1995 J-Store was launched

1995 Project MUSE is a leading provider of digital humanities and social science content for the scholarly community

1997 Consortium of University Research Libraries (CURL)

1997 Greenstone Digital Library Software, produced by the New Zealand Digital Library Project at the University of Waikato, New Zealand

1998 China Academic Library & Information System

1998 WINISIS Distributed in 1995, Version 1.31 launched in November

1999 KOHA, Open Source Integrated Library Management System (ILMS) by Liblime

2000 Software for University Library(SOUL) by INFLIBNET (India)

2000 EPRINTS a Open source Digital Library Software by University of Southampton (School of Electronics and Computer Science)

2001 J-Gate

2001 OAI-PMH version 1.0 was Launched at Washington

2002 DSPACE, Open Repositories Software by MIT and HP labs, United States

2005 NEWGENLIB, Open Source Integrated Library Management Software by Verus Solutions Pvt Ltd (Kesavan Institute of Information and Knowledge Management in Hyderabad, India)